The Paths of Pravritti & Nivritti

1963–2013
GOLDEN JUBILEE

WORLD YOGA CONVENTION 2013
GANGA DARSHAN, MUNGER, BIHAR, INDIA
23rd–27th October 2013

The Paths of Pravritti & Nivritti

Swami Niranjanananda Saraswati

Discourses from the Yogadrishti (Yogavision) series of satsangs at Ganga Darshan Vishwa Yogapeeth, Munger, from 23rd to 26th June 2010

Yoga Publications Trust, Munger, Bihar, India

© Bihar School of Yoga 2011

All rights reserved. No part of this publication may be reproduced, transmitted or stored in a retrieval system, in any form or by any means, without permission in writing from Yoga Publications Trust.

The terms Satyananda Yoga® and Bihar Yoga® are registered trademarks owned by International Yoga Fellowship Movement (IYFM). The use of the same in this book is with permission and should not in any way be taken as affecting the validity of the marks.

Published by Yoga Publications Trust
    First edition 2011
    Reprinted 2013

ISBN: 978-93-81620-01-4

Publisher and distributor: Yoga Publications Trust, Ganga Darshan, Munger, Bihar, India.

Website: www.biharyoga.net
         www.rikhiapeeth.net

Printed at Aegean Offset Printers, Greater Noida

Dedication

*To our guru Sri Swami Satyananda Saraswati
who continues to inspire and guide us
on our spiritual journey.*

Contents

The Traveller's Tale   1

The Path of Pravritti   13

Harmonizing Pravritti, Discovering Nivritti   33

Guru's Guidance   49

The Traveller's Tale

23 June 2010

As many of you know, I closed a chapter of my life in 2009. The major events in that closed chapter have been in relation to yoga and the propagation of yoga in India and overseas. For forty years, under the guidance, inspiration and instruction of my guru, Sri Swami Satyananda Saraswati, I successfully and efficiently maintained a pace in propagating yoga throughout the world. It was a small contribution to the great mission of my guru. In July 2009, Sri Swamiji called me

and said, "Now you have to embark upon another journey and in order to do so, one chapter of your life has to close." That was the public life in which I was interacting with people and society, and propagating yoga at a global level. In the new chapter I have to rediscover the aim and purpose of my life for which I have taken sannyasa.

Last month, I took some time off and travelled out, and some of that time was spent in solitude in the high mountains. While I was there, I contemplated the guidelines and instructions that Sri Swamiji had given to me before his mahasamadhi and I wondered: how do I begin to write the opening statements, the prologue, of my second chapter. During those ruminations, I remembered a story that Sri Swamiji had told me years ago when I was a child.

Mr Atmaram and the City of Light
Once there was a traveller who had been travelling for a long time and had not yet reached his destination. The destined place was far away. The traveller was traversing through ages, times and aeons, trying to reach the end of his journey. The destination was Brahmapuri, City of Light, and the name of the traveller was Mr Atmaram, meaning Mr Soul.

After travelling for so long, Mr Atmaram had begun to feel weary and needed to have a rest, so he began to look for a place where he could take a break, recuperate his energies, wash his clothes, eat good food and prepare himself for the next leg of the journey. Soon he came upon a beautiful five-star hotel named Hotel Samsara or Hotel Earth. When he entered the hotel, he was heartily received by the manager and the staff. The manager of the hotel was Mr Moneyram, assisted by two extremely competent girls called Ms Desire and Ms Infatuation.

Mr Moneyram welcomed the traveller, Mr Soul, into the beautiful hotel and after making enquiries on where he was coming from and what his destination was, he said to the traveller, "The distance to the City of Light is much too great. I don't know if anyone has actually reached that city, but many have come searching for it and many have rested in this hotel. You also rest your tired body and recuperate from your exhaustion. Enjoy life, have a good meal, partake of the ambience of this hotel. I will give you my assistants who will ensure that all your needs are looked after." He told Ms Desire and Ms Infatuation, "Please look after Mr Soul. Give him a nice room. Let him unwind. Give him a nice hot bath. Give him nice food. Take him down to the restaurant and when he feels like some enjoyment, take him to the hotel shops and nightclubs and entertain him. Ensure that he forgets his journey to the City of Light and remains in this hotel for a long time to come."

Ms Desire and Ms Infatuation led the traveller to his room. It was a beautiful room where his bags were placed for him and his tired body was rested. Days went by and he continued to live there in the company of the two beautiful assistants. They would escort him for his meals to the restaurants where he would be given delicious fare from every country and the finest spirits and wines. Everything was available in abundance. Ms Desire and Ms Infatuation ensured that the traveller did not face any inconvenience and received everything desired by him. After the evening meal, they would take him to the discotheque where he met many other friends of the hotel manager: Mr Greed, Mr Avarice, Miss Take, Miss Understanding. They were all having a great time and enjoying great parties. Miss Take, Miss Understanding, Ms Desire and Ms Infatuation became the constant companions of Mr Soul, Mr Atmaram.

Mr Atmaram lived in the hotel for many months. The longer he lived there, the less he remembered that he was a traveller, that he was in the hotel only to rest and still had a journey to complete. Many times in his dreams he would remember that he had to travel to the City of Light. However, upon waking up, in the company of the beautiful associates and friends of the hotel manager, he would forget the dream and again become engrossed in the pleasures of the hotel. Time passed.

One day, another traveller came to the hotel. He took a room where he remained in isolation and solitude. The peculiarity of this traveller was that he would lock himself in the room and not come out, not see anyone, not interact with anyone, no male associate, no female associate, no male friend, no female friend. He was the talk of the hotel. All the residents were saying, "This new traveller is very peculiar. He does not meet with anyone. He does not interact with anyone. He eats his meals in his room by ordering room service, he never even comes out." Ms Avarice, Ms Desire, Ms Infatuation, Mr Greed, Mr Jealousy, Miss Take, Miss Understanding all tried to knock on the door of this new traveller to engage him in conversation and show him the comforts and luxuries the hotel had to offer, but he would not open the door to anybody. Everyone failed.

One day at dusk, Mr Soul was walking through the hotel gardens by the swimming pool and he saw the new traveller also taking an evening stroll there. He approached him and asked, "Who are you? You have been in this hotel for some time, but you have not met with any other resident. You have not come to the parties, you have not gone to the restaurants. You have isolated yourself from everyone. Who are you? What is your name?"

The new traveller said, "My name? People call me The Guide. Maybe that is my name. It is my nature to live alone. I don't like to interact with people. I am happiest when I am all alone." Mr Soul could not figure out who this new traveller was. Why was he saying that he did not enjoy any company? Why did he say that he did not enjoy any association with people of the hotel? Why did he live in isolation and solitude? He asked The Guide, "You say people call you The Guide, but what do you do?"

The Guide said, "My duty, profession and job is to guide travellers to the City of Light, Brahmapuri. It is my duty to remind those travellers who forget their destination, who get waylaid, that they have to reach their destination, and also to show them the path, direct them on that path and

tell them how to reach there." When Mr Soul heard that The Guide was able to lead people to the City of Light, he suddenly remembered that he was also a traveller. He asked The Guide again, "I am also journeying to the City of Light. I have stayed in this Hotel Earth for many months. In fact, I've even forgotten how long I have been here. Can you direct me? Can you guide me? Can you show me the way to reach the City of Light?"

The Guide said, "No problem. I am journeying there tomorrow morning. If you wish to join me, you can come with your bag and baggage and we shall travel together to the City of Light." Mr Soul became extremely happy. He said, "Wonderful! Previously I was travelling alone and I did not know the way. Now I have somebody who will guide me, who will show me the way to the City of Light."

Feeling ecstatic, he went to his room, took out his suitcase, and began to pack. While he was busy packing, there was a knock on the door. He opened the door to see the two beautiful girls, Ms Desire and Ms Infatuation, standing there. They said, "Come, let us go to the party. The band of Five Senses is playing in the discotheque. It is the latest rock band. Let us go and hear the music. Let us go and dance."

Mr Soul said, "Sorry. I am not in the mood to party tonight."

"Why?"

"I'm packing."

"You are packing! For what?"

"I am leaving tomorrow."

"Leaving tomorrow! For where?"

"I am going. I want to begin my travels again. I'm going to go to the City of Light, Brahmapuri."

The two girls began to wail and cry. They said, "How can you do that? We have become your friends. Every resident of this hotel has become your friend. Mr Moneyram will die if he hears that his best friend is leaving him. Mr Greed, Mr Jealousy, Miss Take, Miss Understanding, everyone will be heartbroken because their best friend has left them."

Hearing them wail and cry, Mr Moneyram came running and said, "What happened?" Ms Desire explained to Mr Moneyram, "Our beloved friend has taken the decision to leave in the morning with that new traveller, that funny fellow who does not mingle, interact or communicate with anybody, and they have made a pact to go to Brahmapuri, the City of Light."

Mr Moneyram said to Mr Soul, "Listen, friend. Forget that man who has promised to take you to the City of Light. He has been to this hotel many times and he always picks someone and takes them to destinations unknown. He gives them the idea that he will take them to the City of Light, but I doubt whether he actually takes them there. He has lured many travellers from this hotel and I have never heard from them again. I have my doubts whether The Guide can show you the way to the City of Light. Maybe he is a rogue. Maybe at night, when you are tired and asleep, he will kill you and take your possessions and then come back to this hotel again, in wait for the next traveller to prey upon."

In this way, Mr Moneyram, Ms Desire and Ms Infatuation were able to talk the traveller out of his plans. The traveller also thought, "These people are my well-wishers and they are thinking of my welfare, so I should listen to them. The Guide is an unknown stranger. Maybe he will kill me. Maybe he will mislead me. Maybe I will get lost. I will wait in this hotel till I know for sure that there is a specific path, a defined path that I can take to reach the City of Light."

Mr Atmaram stopped packing and went down to the discotheque to hear the music played by the band of Five Senses. He had nice dances with Miss Take, Miss Understanding and Ms Obsession. He had nice drinks with Mr Anger, Mr Jealousy, Mr Avarice and Mr Greed, and he began to enjoy his life once more. The night passed in singing and dancing. He went to bed in the wee hours and, of course, woke up late. When he went down to the restaurant for a meal, at a corner table sat The Guide, as if waiting. Mr Soul said to himself, "I am not going to that man. He will mislead me again. He will misguide me again. I am happy in this hotel. I am comfortable with my companions. I am content. Let me just avoid Mr Guide." Thinking in this manner, he sat down to have his meal.

Mr Guide saw Mr Soul and came over to his table and said, "What happened? I was waiting for you this morning. At four o' clock I was at the gate of the hotel waiting for you to join me. You did not come." Mr Soul said, "How could I come? How can I leave my friends who love me so much? How can I leave my friends who respect me so much, want me so much, care for me so much, dote on me so much? If I leave, I will break their hearts, the most beautiful hostess, Ms Passion, the assistants of the manager, Ms Desire and Ms Infatuation, who are all very close to me. If I leave, I will break their hearts, they will die. They will pine away in memory of me. I cannot bear the agony of making them suffer."

The Guide was silent for a while. He said, "All right. You want to know the truth about the people who live in this hotel? I will tell you the truth. In this hotel, nobody belongs to anyone. Everyone is a totally independent person. They may say that they love you, but in reality they don't. They may say that they want you and desire you, but in reality they don't. They are here only to confuse you so that you do not undertake the journey to your destination."

Mr Soul said, "How can you say that? I know that Ms Passion loves me very much. I know that Ms Desire dotes on me. I know that Ms Infatuation cares for me. I know that Mr Moneyram is my best friend. How can you say that nobody belongs to anyone in this hotel?"

The Guide said, "You want proof? I will give you proof. Go to your room now and behave normally. Give me one chance to explain to you the futility of staying in this hotel."

The traveller said, "All right. I will do as you say because I want to know the truth."

He went back to his room and awaited the arrival of Ms Desire and Ms Infatuation. They came in the evening and played around with him. They said to him, "You are our best friend, so much so that we want to make you a permanent resident of this hotel. You can become staff like us. Then you can enjoy all the comforts and luxuries of this five-star hotel for all times to come. You can enjoy our company day and night; you can enjoy the company of all your friends here and live your life happily. You belong to us, we belong to you; we cannot live without you. If you go, we shall surely wither and die." After pleasing Mr Soul, at midnight, they left his room.

Mr Soul prepared to go to sleep now that everyone had gone and darkness had fallen on the floor where he was staying. Just then, he heard a knock on the door. He opened the door. Before him stood The Guide. He said, "So you have seen the antics of Ms Desire and Ms Infatuation?" Mr Soul said, "What do you mean? What antics? They were truthful and sincere when they said that they are my friends and that they will die without me. I did not see any antics or manipulation. I did not see any games."

The Guide said, "All right. Come with me." He took Mr Soul to another floor, another room, which was locked from inside. He said, "Listen carefully to what is going on in the room." Mr Soul put his ear to the door and heard the voices of Ms Desire and Ms Infatuation talking with another man. He was disturbed. He took a peep through the keyhole and saw that Ms Desire and Ms Infatuation along with Mr Moneyram and other staff of the hotel were talking to another traveller and telling him that he was their friend and they would die without him if he left the hotel.

Mr Soul was in shock. He turned around to The Guide and said, "Yes, you are right. In this hotel, nobody belongs to anyone. Everyone is looking out for themselves. The same words, the same sentences that Mr Moneyram, Ms Passion, Ms Desire and Ms Infatuation spoke to me, the same actions that they played out before me, they are using them for another traveller. O Guide, you have opened my eyes! Now I understand that in this world, in this hotel, nobody belongs to anyone. I am ready to go with you to the City of Light. Please take me with you."

The Guide came closer and said, "Before we embark on the journey, you have to leave behind everything that has been given to you by Miss Take, Miss Understanding, Ms Desire, Ms Need, Ms Passion. Come, take off your clothes. The glittery shining tuxedo that you are wearing, take it

off", and he gave him two geru dhotis to wear. The Guide said, "Remove all the ornaments and jewellery, the rings, the necklaces that Miss Understanding and Miss Take have given to you", and he gave him a rudraksha mala to wear. The Guide said, "Remove the hair, because hair is a label, an identification with this hotel." After shaving the traveller's head, The Guide said, "Now you are ready to come with me to the City of Light", and they left the hotel at midnight. Leaving behind everything, The Guide and Mr Soul journeyed towards the City of Light, Brahmapuri.

While sitting in the mountains, I was thinking of this story that Sri Swamiji had told me many years ago. I was looking down from the mountains to the plains, and observing how people lived. I saw that people who lived in the plains, in cities and villages, were the travellers living in the hotel called Earth. The Guide comes to them from time to time to say, "If you have had enough of this hotel and are ready to embark on the journey to the City of Light, come with me." But how many actually listen to this call of The Guide, the guru? Not many. Everyone is engrossed in their associations with the staff and manager of the hotel who delude the mind of the traveller whenever the desire to embark on the journey manifests. I thought to myself, "Thanks to the grace of my guru, Ms Desire and Ms Infatuation have stayed away from me. But then, what about all those people who are being deluded by the band of Five Senses and spend their time partying, dancing and singing whenever the band plays? What about those who are associating with Miss Take, Miss Understanding, Ms Desire, Ms Passion and Ms Infatuation? What will happen to them?"

Two paths of life

The answer is: everything depends on how you live your life. The style in which you live your life determines what your aspiration, determination and sankalpa will be.

In our tradition, the sages have defined two paths. One is the path of pravritti and the other is the path of nivritti. The path of pravritti leads you to the dimension of the senses and sense objects and the path of nivritti leads you away from the dimension of the senses and sense objects, towards the City of Light or the transcendental dimension. These are the two paths that every human being has to walk.

The common factor in the two terms, pravritti and nivritti, is vritti. *Vritta* means a circle and *vritti* means the circular movement of the mind. What is the meaning of the circular movement of the mind? When the mind is unable to extract itself from a particular experience, then it is caught in a whirlpool, a vortex, and becomes sucked deeper and deeper into that field of experience. This is known as vritti. When the prefix 'pra' is added and vritti becomes 'pravritti', it means a deep identification, a deep connection with the world of senses and sense objects. When the word 'nivritti' is used, it means disidentification, disconnection with the world of senses and sense objects.

How can you disconnect from the world? For as long as you are a traveller upon earth, you have to use the tools with which you have come. These tools are the body, the senses, the mind, the intellect, the sentiments. You have to utilize the faculties of this equipment to survive, whether to bind yourself in the mire of the world or uplift yourself from it. The tools are the same for both. A person who is totally engrossed in the world is using the body, the senses, the mind and the intellect to survive in the material world, and the person who wants to extract himself from the effects and influences of the material, sensual and sensorial world also has to utilize the same tools of the body, senses, mind and intellect. The tools are the same for a person engrossed and involved in the world of senses and for one who is spiritually enlightened.

Completing the journey

What is it that makes a difference in the understanding and perception of these two groups of people? It is the lifestyle. The way or style in which you live and express your life is what is important in walking the path of either pravritti or nivritti. The path of pravritti leads to bondage and that of nivritti leads to freedom.

What is meant by style of life or lifestyle? There are different lifestyles that people follow in both the paths of pravritti and nivritti, but what is lifestyle? It is an expression of mentality, behaviour and performance. When these three combine together and govern an individual's life, they create a pattern of living, of viewing, perceiving and responding to the world.

You have to understand lifestyle in relation to upliftment of life and deterioration of life. The pravritti path incorporates different styles of living and the nivritti path also involves different styles of living and perceiving the world. Therefore, the term 'lifestyle' indicates that there is always scope to improve the mentality, behaviour and performance in the expression of life. If you feel that you cannot improve your lifestyle, you are stagnating in Hotel Earth. You have lost your direction and clarity. However, if there is even the tiniest inclination that you have the courage, strength, will, motivation and inspiration to change your lifestyle, it is an indication that you can complete your journey to the City of Light. It is this thread that you have to hold on to – the thread of inspiration and motivation, in order to manage the distorted conditions of life. Thus, the story of Mr Atmaram has become the script of the first page in the blank pages of the second chapter of my life.

The Path of Pravritti

24 June 2010

The seers and thinkers have defined two paths on which the journey of life can take place. One is known as the path of pravritti, that which leads towards vrittis, involvement and participation. The other is that of nivritti, which means becoming separate from that process of involvement.

Having come into this world and this body, and being under the influence and sway of the senses and the mind, the feelings and emotions, the natural inclination of the human nature and human personality is to become involved in the outer, sensorial experience. That is common to all, both the saint and the sinner. Upon acquiring the body, the senses and the mind, both become involved in the process which is extroverted, sensorial, emotional, mental, external, gross and physical. The basic starting point for any journey is the pravritti path, no matter who the traveller is.

Pravritti is composed of two words: 'pra' is a prefix indicating existence and emergence, strength and deep involvement, and 'vritti' means a circular motion, a circular effect, or the involved process. Therefore, the pravritti path indicates the journey towards the dimension of the senses and sense objects.

The nature of the world is *nashwara*, transient: that which existed yesterday and will exist tomorrow. Nashwara is not eternal; it is subject to birth and death, to change. When the spirit is born into this world, then all around in life – in the environment, society, world and creation – it experiences transience, not immortality; it experiences birth and death. Caught in this web, whatever you do, the way you live, eat, sleep, think and behave, is under the sway of vrittis.

Ripples of mind
Vrittis are an expression of the mind. The concept of vritti will become clear if you compare life to a lake. Imagine that the waters of the lake are completely still. There is no movement, no ripple of any kind. In those still waters you can see the reflection of the sky, the clouds, the sun, the moon, the stars, the mountains, the trees. The reflection is seen only when the waters of the lake are absolutely calm and still. If it begins to rain and drops of rain fall on the lake, or if a pebble is thrown into the lake, what will happen to the calm and still surface of the lake? Even if a raindrop falls on the lake, at the point where it enters the lake, small concentric circles, or ripples, will be created. Those circles or ripples are vrittis. The more the rainfall, the more disturbed the outer surface of the lake. As the waters become disturbed, you will not be able to see any reflection in it. That is identical to what happens when you interact with the world of the five senses.

The influences of nature, society and company create different ripples in the mind. You are easily influenced by people, situations, circumstances and events, and lose clarity of mind. You get sucked into one particular feeling, experience, desire, obsession, passion, need or greed. The broad vision in relation to life is lost. That is when your viewpoint becomes narrow. The narrower your viewpoint, the more material you become, as you are able to see only that which is highlighted before you, whether it is your need, greed, ambition, mentality or performance. Anything that you are involved in is highlighted. That is the creation of a vritti.

The creation of vrittis takes away the harmony, balance and peace of mind. The mind becomes ordinary, normal, gross and material. All the attributes of the mind such as the intellect, memory and ego are also influenced by the

narrowness of the mind, which indicates intensification of a vritti. There may be many vrittis but when one vritti becomes predominant, it narrows down the mind. Anger is a vritti. If anger is predominant, it will subdue all other vrittis and will be highlighted. It will dominate the mental, sensorial and cerebral behaviour, thoughts, responses and actions. Fear is a vritti. When it overpowers the other less powerful vrittis, the state of fear dominates your mentality, behaviour and performance.

The more engrossed and involved you become in a vritti, the narrower your mental perceptions and faculties. This in turn makes you more material and gross, external and extroverted. You are caught in the vortex of a vritti, which sucks you in.

Yoga says that vrittis have to be managed, not eradicated: *Yogah chittah vritti nirodhaha* – "Management of vrittis is yoga." Not stoppage of vrittis. If you stop the vrittis, there is no reason to live. You may as well leave this body, mind and existence. As long as you possess a body, you are bound by vrittis. As long as you move in this world, you are guided by vrittis. The entire context of life is connected with vrittis. Thus it is said that anyone who enters this world, enters into the maze of vrittis and forgets their real nature, loses clarity, discrimination and wisdom, and acts upon the vrittis. This is the path of pravritti. Just as a house is built of bricks and cement, life and the world are built up of vrittis. Therefore, no one can be free of vrittis and you should not even wish so. The only effort you need to make is to become free of the vrittis that cause downfall and bondage, and cultivate those that uplift. Therefore, it is not stopping the vrittis that yoga aspires for, but managing the vrittis.

When you are driving along a road and there are bumps, holes and rocks, you continue to drive, but carefully. You do not oppose or resist the bumpy road; the journey does not stop in spite of the road. As the road becomes more difficult and constricted, you become more alert and try to complete the journey with greater awareness. When the road is clear, you accelerate in fourth gear. The same principle needs to be applied to the mind. When there is some kind of spike in the mind, whether due to anxiety or joy, you have to become aware of everything in and around and take the car forward slowly. The anxiety, sorrows and joys are the bumps. You go up, go down and come up again. Therefore, you need to drive your mind in life the way you drive a car on a bumpy road. You have to know the reason why vrittis are created within you and how they connect you with the world of senses and sense objects, and remain free from their influence, which dilutes the clarity, strength and positive qualities of the mind.

In the path of pravritti you are simply following the trail of vrittis, and lose the ability to exercise *sanyam*, restraint, and *anushasana*, discipline. Life is marked by the absence of restraint and discipline.

Whims of indiscipline

If you look at your life objectively, at how you live, you will discover that there is no system. You are only following the whims of the mind. There is no structure, regularity, system or discipline. Everyone is following the whims of their mind: "I want to sleep at this time, I want to get up at this time. I want to eat this, I don't like this, I like that. I want to associate with this person, that person is my enemy. I have my own needs, my own ambitions." That is your world.

Your world is the whimsical nature of your own self. Likes and dislikes, jealousy, anger, hatred and greed are all whims of the mind. What you want to wear today is a whim of the mind, what you want to eat today is a whim of the mind, and the nature of a whim is expressing itself to impress others.

You are always seeking to impress others so that you are recognized as somebody special. This is everyone's quest: recognition. Friendship, companionship and recognition are the three things the society gives and every individual looks for in society. They only fulfil the whims of the mind. This is how you have been living.

There is no structure in your life. Today you sleep at ten o'clock, tomorrow at twelve o'clock. On another day you party the whole night and sleep during the day. Another day, you splurg on things that are totally unnecessary to your survival. You do not care when you rise, when you sleep, when you eat, when you work. You do everything based on your whims. If you feel like it, you may do something; if you don't feel like it, you won't. If the thought comes into your mind, you will go by it. If a thought comes, 'Don't do it', you won't do it. This means that you simply follow whatever the mind says. If the mind calls something good, you will agree. If it calls something bad, you will accept that. When you cannot discriminate between good and bad and do not have any choice in the matter, it means that you are stuck in a vritti and are being sucked deeper into it. You are creating associations based on your mind, of like and dislike, acceptance and rejection. You develop your own identity and idea of what is appropriate and inappropriate. Each idea, each behaviour is being guided by a particular vritti. In a life where there is absolutely no structure, no system, no discipline, in which you are always moving in the direction of the sensory pleasures and fulfilment, how can you develop balance?

You know and understand many things, but cannot put them into practice. Why? Due to vrittis, which influence you because you identify with the world and are connected with the world. The stronger this connection, the further you move away from sanyam, anushasana, peace and balance. Sri Swamiji often says that the nature of the mind is like that of a monkey. A monkey can never sit still. It will climb a tree, pluck a fruit, take one bite and throw it away. It will always jump from one tree to another, picking fruit after fruit without eating any one fruit fully. In the same way, you keep running after different desires in order to attain them. You advance a little in your attempt and then doubt arises: 'Will I be able to finish this task?', and you are unable to accomplish it and regress. The human mind is like a monkey because it is caught in the circles of vrittis.

There are two kinds of vrittis: joyful and painful. A joyous circumstance gives birth to a joyous vritti and a painful circumstance gives birth to a painful vritti. Even when you experience joy, there is no balance or restraint in it. The same is true of pain. You are dragged by the force of both currents.

The path of pravritti is the path of the world. It is the path of agitation, chaos and confusion. This is a path where you connect with the senses and desire the pleasures of the senses. Every person is desirous of sense pleasure; everyone tries to please the mind at the material level. If there is any problem in life, in your body, society, house or family, you become engrossed in that problem. Becoming engrossed means that you move away from peace and balance, and live only through that experience. You go on experiencing that situation internally, either congratulating or cursing yourself because of it. If there is happiness, you congratulate yourself; if there is pain, you curse yourself. These are the vrittis of the world and you live them. Every day you live lust, anger, envy, hatred, like, dislike. Is anyone free of them? This indicates that you are caught up in the world, that you are only involved in conducting your dealings with the world. Where there is lack of restraint and discipline, you cannot attain peace and happiness. Instead, you have to face anarchy and disorder, whether outside or inside.

Material life, which is represented by the objects and desires of the world, inspires you to live a certain kind of lifestyle: the normal lifestyle which you live at home. Just observe the situation in your own house: when do people go to sleep and wake up, what do they eat and not eat, what do they wear and not wear, what desires do they express, what kind of hatred and love do they carry within. If you look at your own family members, you will see the full force of materialism. One person says, "I don't like this", another person says, "I like that very much." The material world is dictating their behaviour, thought and mentality completely. Like and dislike are manifestations of the world. Wanting to wear good clothes, eating good food, living a good life – all these are dictates of the world. These are images of the world, reflected by your mind in the form of your whims and desires.

Lessening intensity of vrittis

From the yogic perspective, in order to develop balance, you have to cultivate discipline and restraint in life. Restraint plus discipline equals sadhana. Sadhana does not mean performing postures or practising meditation. They are methods and tools that you can use to create a change within your nature, character and life. The tool can be pranayama, asana, meditation, pratyahara, dharana, mantra, and so on. They are not sadhanas, they are tools which are used in order to acquire discipline, create a structure and learn restraint in life. Therefore, restraint plus discipline plus tool equals sadhana.

In the material, extroverted or external dimension the qualities that emerge are tamasic and rajasic, not sattwic. A human being does not hold sattwa in life. If you think you have sattwa, you are grossly mistaken. There is no scope for sattwa in your life, as you are caught in the pulls of vrittis. There are people who wish to see God, who wish to experience the divine nature, but they are unable to relate in a good, positive or healthy way with those around them. Can such a person ever be a devotee? Never! If you cannot manage your behaviour, forget about God. If you cannot manage your own responses of vrittis, forget about peace and shanti. That is the truth that you ignore and hide away from. If you cannot treat your fellow human being who is sitting beside you with a smile, happiness and joy, then don't have any expectation of being a devotee or experiencing the divine nature in your life.

The gunas of tamas and rajas guide the pravritti path. Sattwa guna does not guide the pravritti path, it guides the nivritti path. As you become more entangled in vrittis, the tamasic qualities manifest. As you develop more vrittis, the rajasic qualities manifest. When tamas and rajas are predominant, your behaviour and mind are also rajasic and tamasic, aggressive, manipulative, seeking power, trying to control and manipulate, trying to project yourself. If there is a threat to any condition of your security, these qualities become active.

Your lifestyle in society, influenced by vrittis, is rajasic and tamasic. When the lifestyle is rajasic, desire after desire takes birth in the mind. You think of name and fame as the basis of life. Recognition by another person becomes the basis of your life. If you do a good job and another person does not even look at it, you feel 'I did such a splendid job and it was not even recognized!' This is a result of the rajasic lifestyle. In the tamasic lifestyle, you do not want to come out of the condition in which you feel secure. You behave like a frog in a well. You do not search for any change or the possibility of becoming better. You say, "I am happy as I am."

In the pravritti path, you oscillate between rajas and tamas. Your lifestyle is inspired by the conditions of these two gunas. Desires, karmas and thoughts are born, but they are all connected with transitory pleasure and not with searching for the inner spirit. The pravritti path is the worldly path in which there is no restraint or discipline, system or peace. It is empty.

Let us ask those who have completed fifty orbits around the sun, "Has there been any change in the ambitions and desires that you had when you were twenty-five compared to now?" Many will say no and some will say yes. The reply will be based on how you view life or your expectations from life. If you have had many expectations and desires and wanted to achieve a lot at the material level, whether name, fame or prosperity, you will say, "No, there is no difference." You will have the same drive and motivation to achieve that you did at twenty-five. Some people will say, "Yes, there has been a decrease." They are those who have taken the beatings of life and have come to an understanding of what is appropriate and inappropriate for them, and how to go towards one and avoid the other. Such people are able to say, "Yes, there is a difference between twenty-five and fifty. There is a difference in the intellect, thinking, understanding, expectations and ambitions." Nevertheless, both kinds of people are walking the pravritti path.

Everyone in this world is walking the pravritti path. Therefore, you have to ask how you can continue to walk it,

yet cultivate positivity and sattwa. You have to find out how you can free yourself from the rajasic and tamsic vrittis and make room for sattwic vrittis in your life. You need to think about how the state of tamas and rajas in the pravritti path can be transformed into a state of sattwa. You live in society and the world. You have your job or profession. You have your family. They all have their own expectations, beliefs and thinking. You also have your own behaviour and personality to contend with. Taking them all into consideration, how can you take your life towards sattwa?

The wise people have provided a sutra. They say, there are twenty-four hours in a day. Give twenty-three to the world and keep one for your own upliftment. In those twenty-three hours, do whatever you have to in the world, but keep that one hour for self-observation and decide upon a sadhana which you will practise during that period. If you can do this, then despite walking the pravritti path, you will be able to create a sattwic way of thinking, behaviour and attitude. That will be the biggest achievement of your pravritti life.

The sattwic quality is an attempt to gradually transform and transmute the negative effects of tamas and rajas, and that is possible when sadhana is incorporated into one's life.

The seers and yogis have said that yes, it is possible to lessen the intensity of the tamasic and rajasic qualities in life and to do so, you have to go through different processes of sadhana, the first being learning restraint and cultivating discipline. If there is no sadhana, restraint, discipline or proper application of the tools, sattwa cannot come into your life.

Three levels of restraint

The tradition says that restraint has to be observed on three levels. The first is speech restraint, the second is mind restraint and the third is sensorial restraint.

Speech restraint: Speech is the medium through which interaction is conducted. It reflects the state and condition of the mind. If the mind is negative, the speech will be negative. If the mind is positive, the speech will be positive. Speech is a reflection of whatever you experience in the mind. If you are mentally disturbed or agitated, that will be evident in your speech. Speech is a reflection of mental behaviour. It is a gross expression of the subtle mental state.

In order to manage mental behaviour through speech, it is said that speech has to be truthful as well as pleasant. People love growling at each other. To cultivate pleasant speech, remember not to growl at anybody. Pleasant speech means that your words should not harm or disturb the mind of the person to whom they are addressed.

There is a story of a king who wanted to know his future. He gave his birth chart to an astrologer and said, "Tell me what you see in it."

The astrologer looked at the chart and thought to himself, 'This is a very bad chart.' He said to the king, "O king, in your chart I see the death and destruction of your empire; I see the death and destruction of your kith and kin. I see the decline of your empire." The king was furious. He said, "How dare you say all this? I am at the peak of my power and you are predicting the destruction of my entire clan? The decline of my empire? Throw this astrologer in the jail!" The astrologer was put in jail.

The king now called another astrologer. The second man also saw the same future in the chart, but he knew what had happened to his predecessor. He thought about it and then said, "O king! I have never seen a chart like yours. This is the best chart I have ever seen. You will outlive everyone. You have a very long life. You will outlive even your grandsons."

The king was delighted to hear this and gave bountiful rewards to the second astrologer. Now, this man had said the same thing as the first astrologer, but in a different way. The first one said, "I see death and destruction" and was put in prison. The second one said, "I see longevity" and was rewarded. Both said the same thing, but the language used was different.

That is the effect of *vani*, speech. You experience this every day. If somebody abuses you, how do you react? If somebody praises you, how do you react? A stranger can come up to you and say, "You are wonderful", and you will feel happy. A stranger can come up to you and say, "You are hopeless, you are ugly, you are horrible", and you will descend into depression. That is the power of speech. That is the effect speech can have on the mind. It is not that only the words of your friends will make an impact on you. Even the words of strangers have an effect.

The way to acquire speech sanyam is to cultivate the two qualities of pleasantness and truthfulness. Pleasantness, *priyata*, and truthfulness, *satyata*, are the tools which one can use to acquire *vani sanyam* or speech restraint. It is a sadhana applicable to everyone. Try it and you will be the winner.

In normal day-to-day situations, apply restraint of speech in every interaction. In the ashram, mouna is practised at certain times. Some people believe that mouna means not to speak at all. That is one way to start off the journey of mouna. However, the word *mouna* does not actually mean silence; it means measured speech. That is the literal definition. It is derived from the root 'mapa', which means to measure. But as you don't know how to measure your speech, it is better to zip up the lips and remain silent. After all, what do you speak about? Most of the time, you only indulge in gossip and criticism, all negative expressions. You only try to satisfy your sensory cravings through speech. Such speech has no power or meaning. Analyze the sentences that you speak every day – how many are worthwhile and how many are absolutely useless, critical and gossipy in nature? Undertake an objective analysis of your own speech, and you will be surprised. Maybe out of a hundred sentences, ten were necessary and the remaining ninety were useless. Not everyone is capable of knowing what appropriate speech is. Therefore, their practice of measured speech must begin with absolute silence. When you have been a bit observant and are able to observe and filter the essence of your thoughts and convert them into speech, you can begin to practise measured speech.

When you edit a book, certain words and sentences are crossed out and others are added. You go on editing a sentence until you are satisfied that it conveys the right meaning. In the same way, you have to edit what you speak. Before speaking, edit what you are about to say. That is mouna and that is measured speech. In this process of editing, bring in the component of satyata, truthfulness, and priyata, pleasantness. In this way, vani sanyam can be practised at any time, in any interaction or communication.

Another aspect of speech restraint is clarity of speech. Think whether the person you are addressing is able to understand what you are saying. When there is clarity in speech, there is clarity in behaviour also. That is why The Guide in the story of 'City of Light' did not meet anyone. He preferred to live in solitude, believing:

Hara hala mein alamasta sacchidananda hoon;
Chidananda, chidananda, chidananda hoon.

In every circumstance I am intoxicated;
I am truth-consciousness-bliss;
Consciousness-bliss am I, consciousness-bliss am I,
consciousness-bliss am I.

The traveller who went out of his room and spoke to everyone became deluded, as the thought waves of others influenced him. Humans may be embodied beings, but our essence is energy. What we say and think spreads around like waves. The thought that is arising in your mind right now is spreading everywhere in the form of waves. Radio waves exist in the atmosphere, but they are not visible. You need a special instrument to catch them – a radio. You also need to turn its dial around to get the right station. Only then do the radio waves emerge in the form of audible words. If you do not possess a radio, however, you cannot say that radio waves don't exist.

I recall a small incident. Once, we were travelling with Sri Swamiji. We hailed a taxi and our group of three or four sannyasins jumped in. The taxi driver was an atheist. At first he wasn't very happy to see sannyasins occupying his taxi, but after we had travelled a little distance he opened up and initiated a conversation: "Where have you come from? What do you do? I have seen many sannyasins. They all deceive each other and rob ordinary people." He went on talking and said, "All these sannyasins believe in God. I don't believe in God. I haven't seen him to this day; therefore I don't believe that he exists. If he existed, then we would have been able to see him. For so many thousands of years people have been trying to see God, but nobody has been successful. All this is lies. It is all nonsense. Am I right or wrong, Swamiji?"

Sri Swamiji remained quiet for some time. Then he said, "You are right. Whatever your view, it is right for you. But reply to a question of mine. Have you ever seen a radio wave?" The driver remained silent. Sri Swamiji said, "But you can experience it when you turn on a radio. The same applies to God. God is a wave which you cannot see, but if you fine-tune or adjust your mind, you will be able to receive that wave. You will be able to experience and feel God's existence."

Everything that you experience in life is a wave. After all, what is joy? Joy also has a wave form which you experience in the mind and the senses. What is pain? It may be a circumstance externally, but its experience is in the form of a

wave which is influencing your mind and emotions. Tamas, rajas and sattwa are terms that are used to describe the gunas, but they are experienced as waves. You send out waves into the world and the world sends out waves to you. This exchange of waves is the mind, but its gross expression is speech. Therefore, the first step in speech restraint is ensuring that your words do not cause misunderstanding or harm anyone. Thus it has been said: *Satyam bruyaat, priyam bruyaat* – "Speak the truth, speak what is pleasant." One who can practise truth and pleasantness in speech is able to acquire speech restraint.

Mental restraint: The second form of restraint is mental restraint. You have to remember to observe the mind in order to acquire mental restraint. The best way to observe the mind is not observing the thoughts or the activities taking place in the mind, but knowing your weaknesses and ambitions, strengths and needs.

Strengths represent the sattwic qualities or positive forces of life. Weaknesses represent the tamasic qualities, the limitations and conditions which you are unable to transcend. Ambitions represent the rajasic qualities, the desires which motivate you. Needs are a balance of all three.

In the usual involvement with vrittis, you are more aware of the limitations, the tamasic quality, and the ambitions, the rajasic quality. In the course of the journey through life, ambitions always remain highlighted in the mind. The rajasic quality is always predominant because that is what is motivating you continuously. That is your drive. However, when you are unable to acquire what you desire due to certain limitations or constraints, you become acutely aware of those limiting factors, the tamasic quality, and they pull you down into depression and dejection, into believing that you are not an achiever.

Thus, the mind has to be seen in terms of strengths, weaknesses, ambitions and needs. Every individual has certain strengths which they are identified with. Your strengths will be visible in your mode of work and thinking, and that enables others to come to a conclusion about your state of mind. If you are able to cultivate the strengths of mind, you are increasing the level of sattwa. You are invoking the qualities which will help you progress in life.

Weaknesses define your limits – that which you cannot cross over. Think, what are the weaknesses of your life and to what extent do they sway you? If insecurity, anxiety for the future or intense passions continuously overwhelm you, then tamo guna predominates in your life. These weaknesses do not allow evolution of life and limit you within certain boundaries. Limitations and weaknesses are tamasic. They define the limit of your participation and involvement; you are unable to go beyond them. When you identify with a limitation, you become tamasic and when you identify with strength of character, you become sattwic.

In the same way, another state of mind reflects ambition. Everyone has certain ambitions, whether in respect to their own self, family or society. However, caught up in the whirlpool of worldly vrittis, often you are unable to discern whether an ambition is beneficial or harmful. An ambition can also become your entire goal in life, and that is when you are sucked even deeper into worldly vrittis. Awareness of aspirations and ambitions is manifestation of the rajasic nature: "This is my ambition. Even if it is the last thing I do, I am going to achieve it." Such self-projection and aggression is rajasic.

Needs are basic to everyone's life, whether a saint or a sinner. The basic needs are shelter, food and clothes, which represent the security that every individual requires. Whether you are a saint, king or beggar, you need all three. Any attempt to fulfil these needs is an indication of the three gunas in a state of harmony. However, when you identify with an ambition, you become rajasic; when needs become ambition, they become rajasic. You need clothing, but when you desire only branded clothes because they are fashionable, that is rajo guna. You need shoes, but when you will settle only for a Nike, that is rajo guna. Need is a state of harmony in the gunas, but when ambition becomes attached to it, it becomes rajasic.

The four conditions of strength, weakness, ambition and need cause ripples in the quiet state of the mind and then influence the mind in the form of vrittis. Therefore, the first step in the process of mental restraint is to identify them. Recognize them, realize them and then manage them. Management or acquisition of mental restraint takes place through meditation. In the twenty-four hours of your daily life, devote at least one hour regularly to your sadhana. Twenty-three hours are for following the world, the senses and sense objects. At this time, forget everything else other than fulfilling what you need to, but use the last remaining hour for introspection, reflection, observation, analysis, modification and transformation.

Mental restraint has to become a meditative process. Observe the rajo guna tendencies of the mind or the ambitions. Observe the sattwa guna tendencies of the mind or the strengths. Observe the tamo guna tendencies of the mind or the weaknesses. See which guna or tendency is predominant and how you can compensate for that negative tendency by bringing in another positive tendency. Thus, mental restraint is a process of self-observation, self-analysis, self-reflection and a need to transform and change. This comes about through meditation, not meditation as defined in the sequence of pratyahara, dharana and dhyana, but a simple meditation in which you close your eyes and begin to see yourself and your mind. You observe it and try to recognize and become aware of what is actually needed to change a quality, character or behaviour of the mind, and adopt that in your life.

Sense restraint: The third restraint is *indriya sanyam*, restraint of the senses. The senses are always seeking their own gratification. The eyes like to see what is pleasant to them, the ears like to hear what is pleasant to them, the tongue likes to taste what is pleasant to it, the skin likes to touch what is pleasant to it, the nose likes to smell what is pleasant to it. All the senses are seeking self-gratification.

There would be no harm in seeking self-gratification if there was no other option. However, as a human being you do have another option, which is to contain and restrict the involvement of the senses with sense objects. That is possible only through *jnana*, wisdom, through acquiring a concept of what is just and appropriate. This is not easy. For instance, people who suffer from illnesses such as diabetes have to follow certain dietary restrictions. They cannot eat rice, potatoes or sweets, but it is often difficult for them to control the urge to eat those things. They think, "I have taken my insulin injection today, I am sure I can allow myself one sweet. I am sure I can allow myself the indulgence of potatoes. I am sure I can eat some rice."

A peculiar desire surfaces to indulge in that which is prohibited, and you are unable to eliminate it. That is because you lack sensory discipline. You lack the mental conviction and sankalpa shakti. Therefore, the senses can sway you at any time. If you possessed sankalpa shakti and restraint, twenty inviting plates of sweets could be before you but you would not try to find a justification for picking even one sweet because you know that they will further damage your system.

There are many things the senses crave and you like to follow these whims of the senses. However, in order to evolve, you have to come to the point where you are able to control the senses through your wisdom and sankalpa shakti, and say, "Thank you for your advice, but I have another thought."

Restraint of the senses, speech and mind are the three steps that begin the awakening of the positive forces and counteract the negative influences of vrittis. Restraint, along with discipline, is a sadhana of life.

Living systematically
There has to be a system and structure in your day-to-day activities. If there is a nice movie playing on television, you will stay up till one o'clock watching it. If there is a party, you will go there and stay up the whole night. As for food habits, whether you are hungry or not, you will munch on something if you feel like it because food is available to you in plenty. Open the refrigerator door at any time and enjoy. Your fridge is stacked with a choice of drinks, snacks and food and you constantly indulge in them. In fact, the choices are so many that people now live to eat rather than eat to live, and they also love to eat.

Anushasana or discipline means creation of a system in the normal routine of life. There must be a time to sleep, to rise, to eat, not to eat, to work and to relax. The word *anushasana* is composed of two words: 'anu' meaning subtle and 'shasana' meaning to govern or rule. Therefore, what is called discipline in English is called anushasana in Sanskrit, its literal meaning being acquiring the ability to control the subtle behaviours of one's nature.

Acquiring the ability to control the subtle behaviour of your character, personality or nature indicates that you can avoid tension. Tension is a subtle manifestation of the mind over which you do not have any control. If the mind is agitated, there is tension; if desires are not fulfilled, if you do not have food or clothes, there is tension. What is called tension in the broad sense is actually a subtle expression of the mind. These subtle expressions distort the mind, cloud the intellect and destroy peace. Tension need not be conscious; it can also be subconscious and unconscious, affecting the entire personality, body, mind and emotions. Once there is tension, peace and happiness disappear from life.

When the subtle behaviour is recognized, you are able to see its effect and how it is causing tension. By creating a system and a structure, you eliminate the causes of tension. Elimination of tension is yoga; learning how to manage subtle tensions is another definition of yoga.

Being able to manage subtle tensions allows you to rule and govern your nature and personality, and become the master of your own life. Becoming the master of your life means *Tadah drashtuh swaroope avasthanam* – "Then you are established in your own nature." (*Yoga Sutras*, 1:3)

In the pravritti path, the aim of sadhana is acquisition of a structure, system, discipline and restraint which will lead to the lessening of tamasic and rajasic qualities and allow cultivation of the sattwic character. With cultivation of the sattwic character, you become motivated to discover the inner dimension and begin the journey in the nivritti path.

Harmonizing Pravritti, Discovering Nivritti

25 June 2010

The two paths of life are pravritti and nivritti. The path of pravritti leads towards the world and the path of nivritti leads towards transcendence. In the pravritti path, you are engrossed and involved in the experience of the senses and the sense objects, and every action in life is performed under the sway of vrittis. There is lack of restraint and discipline, and everything is based on the whims of the mind. If the whims are not satisfied, there is pain, unhappiness and depression.

Since everyone living in society follows the pravritti path, you need to understand how to inculcate discipline and restraint while walking this path. The basic requirement to be uplifted spiritually and internally for a person involved in this path is attainment of restraint and discipline. These are the biggest accomplishments for a worldly person. The concept of restraint includes restraint of speech, restraint of mind and restraint of the senses.

Practising restraint

Acquiring truthfulness and pleasantness: In order to acquire restraint of speech, the two tools that are used are truthfulness and pleasantness. The speech, communication and behaviour of every individual must be truthful as well as pleasant. When there is truth and pleasantness, the speech is full of energy and purity, and is used for your own upliftment as well as that of others.

Words are waves of energy which affect the mind and emotions. If someone speaks words of praise, you feel happy. If someone speaks words of abuse, you are pained. The play of words brings about the experiences of pain and pleasure because words hold power, and truthfulness and pleasantness in speech enhance this power.

Falsity and unpleasantness come into life when you are caught up in the web of tamasic and rajasic qualities. Making an attempt to acquire truthfulness and pleasantness is difficult initially, but these are the tools that empower your words, your speech, and allow you to acquire restraint of speech.

Identifying sattwa: The mind is a subtle and vast area of experience. To acquire restraint of mind, the first step is becoming aware of your strengths, weaknesses, ambitions and needs. The strengths represent the positive or sattwic quality in life. Identification with positive qualities and strengths indicates an optimistic nature, a mind which is guided by hope, and is creative and positive. It indicates a person who is open-minded and discriminative.

In everyday life, the emergence of sattwa is seen when you identify with positive qualities and strengths. It is always said in yoga that instead of worrying about the negative, the limiting and the destructive, identify with that which is positive, constructive and sattwic. This will ultimately elevate the consciousness from the gross to the transcendental. Cultivation of strengths is, therefore, enhancement of the sattwic nature.

Getting a grip on tamas: The next step is identifying weaknesses, the limitations and restrictions which are self-imposed, or the possibilities that have not been recognized due to lack of maturity of mind. The limitations represent the tamasic qualities and nature. By identifying these limiting, restrictive and weak conditions of life, you are actually identifying the tamasic areas of your life which inhibit or restrict your growth and progress, and do not allow you to reach your goal and attain the peace and contentment that you desire.

The reason for not being able to acquire positivity in life is only one: you have forgotten your capabilities due to the grip of tamas, and the weaknesses have become stronger. Therefore, identification of weaknesses is important. At the same time, cultivation of positive strengths is also necessary. Identifying and recognizing the limitations, restrictions and weaknesses is important to understand the grip of tamas on your nature, but cultivating the right, optimistic and positive qualities is the sadhana that one needs to practise.

Realizing the force of rajas: Identifying your expectations, aspirations and ambitions is necessary to realize the thrust of the rajasic quality in your life. Ask yourself, "In which direction is my rajasic nature taking me, towards destruction or towards upliftment?" If the expectations, ambitions and aspirations in life are not attainable but there is an intense internal craving for them, you will end up in worry and descend into a space of depression and dejection. However, if an aspiration or ambition is attainable, you will begin to connect with the environment, the world and your own spirit. Many times unattainable ambitions become the aim of life and you are unable to complete the journey. If your ambitions are realistic, you can fulfil them and walk on.

As for needs, they represent harmony of the gunas, and the basic needs of food, shelter and clothes are common to all.

Realization of the gunas and mental behaviour takes place only in meditation, when you are able to reflect upon, witness and analyze yourself, your expressions, needs and aspirations. This is not the step by step meditation of pratyahara, dharana and dhyana taught in yoga. It is a method of self-observation and self-analysis; it is a method to know yourself.

Seeing the other side of the coin: The third form of restraint is sensorial restraint. The senses are always craving for something pleasant. The search of the senses is only for pleasure and happiness. The main function of the five *karmendriyas*, organs of action, and the five *jnanendriyas*, organs of knowledge, is to provide a pleasant input to the mind. In this search for a pleasant input, the mind is often distracted from its journey to express its full potential, its actual goal.

According to yoga, cultivation of an opposite thought, *pratipaksha bhavana*, is important to restrain the senses. If the eyes are attracted to something, then create a thought, 'This is nice, but the opposite is also nice.' If the eyes are craving beauty, the mind should also accept the ugly. In this way, the sensory attractions have to be balanced by cultivating awareness of the opposite and not just identifying with that which is pleasurable and offers fleeting joy. The ability to realize both the good and the bad must be developed because they are two sides of the same coin. When one side is being seen, the other side is waiting to be turned over. Once the side turns, what you were seeing goes down and what you have not seen comes up. Therefore, awareness of both the positive and the negative has to be achieved to attain indriya sanyam.

Personal system of discipline

Restraint is one aspect of attaining harmony in the path of pravritti, and the other aspect is discipline. Discipline must be practised with respect to body, mind, diet and sleep to acquire physical, mental and emotional health. In particular, there has to be a proper structure and system to sleep and diet. If you are able to manage these two, all imbalances of life will disappear. Create a system and timing for when you sleep, when you wake up, what you eat, when you eat and why you eat. Such an approach, combined with practices that enhance physical and psychological wellbeing and health, will bring discipline into your daily life.

The method which the yogis discovered for attaining discipline is yoga. With the help of yoga one can attain holistic wellbeing. The imbalances of the body are removed and physical health is acquired; the tensions of the mind are removed and mental peace is attained; the agitation of the emotions is quietened and the emotions are purified; the dissipation of the pranas is checked and they are focused on one point. In this way, when the body, mind, emotions and pranas are controlled with the help of a method, the imbalances and diseases in all these areas are removed automatically and one attains optimum health.

Three mantras: Apart from yoga practices, certain other sadhanas are also essential for developing positivity of mind. Upon waking up in the morning, practise the three mantras: Mahamrityunjaya mantra eleven times, Gayatri mantra eleven times and the thirty-two names of Durga three times. Practising these three mantras creates positive willpower in the mind. They must be practised immediately upon waking up, before you are fully conscious. Many people say that in order to practise any form of concentration, meditation, mantra or any other spiritual practice, one should be totally fresh, awake and alert, and first have a bath. Chanting of mantras is the only exception. Do them before you are fully conscious and up and active.

Mantras need to access the unconscious and subconscious mind. When you wake up in the morning, you are not fully conscious nor are you asleep. You are in that in-between state of subconscious awareness. A lot has been said about the power of the subconscious mind. Whatever thought enters this state of mind will take the form of a *sankalpa*, resolve, and bring about a change in your life, in your mentality, perceptions, attitudes and behaviour. Yoga recognizes this power of positive transformation. Therefore, it is advised that as soon as you wake up, before you even put your foot down the bed, sit down for a few minutes with eyes closed. It is no problem if you are half asleep, that is the right state. In that state of semi-wakefulness and semi-sleep, make a sankalpa for physical health and wellbeing and chant the Mahamrityunjaya mantra eleven times. When you finish it, make a sankalpa for cultivation of wisdom, creativity and positivity in life and chant the Gayatri mantra eleven times. After completing the Gayatri mantra, again make a sankalpa to be free from all distresses of life, whether external or internal, social or personal. Make a sankalpa, "I shall be free from every kind of distress in life", and chant the thirty-two names of Durga, the Cosmic Shakti. That is the end of the mantra practice in the morning.

To practise the three mantras will take about seven to ten minutes at the most, but it is an investment worth making to ensure that the strength, positivity and creativity of the mind are maintained. Normally, when you wake up the first thing you do is reach out for the newspaper or turn on the television. This makes sure that restlessness takes root and negative thoughts start to form, as what you read or see at this time influences the subconscious mind. It is necessary that at this hour you connect with your inherent potential, which is possible with the chanting of the three mantras. This positive awareness which you evoke in yourself in the morning will guide your activities during the day. It will guide your mental behaviour during the day and not allow the mind to be sucked into the dark spaces which one confronts in times of frustration, anxiety, dejection and different mood swings. Therefore, in the system of discipline, the first method is a short practice of mantras to maintain mental positivity, harmony and balance during the day.

Asana and pranayama: For physical wellbeing, choose a few asanas and pranayamas. The tradition speaks of 84,000 asanas. Out of these, eighty-four are important. Out of these eighty-four, five are important for a normal person. For a person suffering from a debilitating condition, depending on what the condition is, one has to pick a different combination of asanas and pranayamas and other allied supportive techniques. For a normal, healthy person who simply wants to maintain the wellbeing, health and stamina of the body, only five practices are important to ensure that the pranas are flowing properly throughout the body. They are: tadasana, tiryaka tadasana, kati chakrasana, surya namaskara and sarvangasana. There is no need to practise any other yoga posture beyond these five. If you do them regularly, you will never suffer from any physical problem, illness, disease or impairment in the performance of the internal body systems. These asanas will ensure that the internal systems are maintained properly, and the body remains supple and energetic.

In addition, two pranayamas must be practised: nadi shodhana and bhramari. Nadi shodhana balances the two brain hemispheres. There are two hemispheres of the brain, the left and the right. In the right hemisphere there is nothing left, and in the left hemisphere there is nothing right! Nadi shodhana pranayama balances the two and removes nervous tensions. Bhramari regulates the functions of the endocrine system. When the functions of the glandular systems are regulated and the brain is charged with oxygen and prana shakti and its two hemispheres are working in coordination, then the efficiency of the brain and mind increases manifold.

Thus, five asanas and two pranayamas are necessary for creating a system of physical discipline while the three mantras are necessary for a system of mental discipline.

Yoga nidra: Whenever you feel tired during the day, do a short practice of yoga nidra. At any time when the body, muscles, mind and brain feel tired, yoga nidra will revive you. This is because when tiredness is removed from body and mind, the pranas are activated and you feel energized once again.

Bedtime meditation: Meditation is necessary to de-stress at night. If you are able to de-stress yourself before going to sleep, in the course of time your whole personality will change, as the biggest problem in life is stress.

Everyone suffers from stress and you are not able to manage it. Stress is always accumulated and you are unable to release the accumulated stress. Meditation can be used as a tool to de-stress before going to sleep at night. This will allow the mind to become relaxed and be at peace with itself. It will not be influenced by the intense vrittis. The mind identifies with vrittis only at times of stress. When there is no stress, when you are totally relaxed, then the mind has the ability to stand back and look at all the vrittis and its involvement with the world of senses and sense objects objectively. Therefore, meditation should be practised at night before going to sleep, even if for five minutes. For these five minutes, separate yourself from the world. Say to yourself, "I am free from the influences of the world. I am not the mind, nor the experiences of pain and pleasure connected with the mind. I am not the body, nor the experiences of pain and pleasure associated with the body. I am the conscious spirit." Invoking this thought, for five minutes practise any method of meditation. One mala of mantra, thought observation or mind observation, any system of pratyahara or dharana can be adopted. Then go to sleep.

In this way, you can create a structure, system and discipline to release the stresses and tensions of the mind through meditation, ensure that the pranas and energies of the body flow properly with the practice of asanas and pranayamas, and that the mind remains centred, focused and positive with the chanting of the mantras. This is acquisition of personal discipline.

Dietary regulation: External discipline constitutes dietary discipline and sleep discipline. Psychologists, psychiatrists and psychoanalysts say that when there is some kind of mental, psychological or emotional problem which you are unable to work out, then the craving for food enhances and you consume more. Eating is not a problem. The after-effect of not eating properly is the bigger problem.

The physical system is controlled and regulated by the flow of hormones and other chemicals. When you eat, the digestive juices that are released do not differentiate between the different quantities of food that you eat. Whether you eat a complete meal or a single peanut, the quantity of digestive juices released will always be the same. Every time that you eat, you are flushing your system with hormones and chemicals which can create problems when not eliminated. Bile is a result of this condition. The bilious nature of the body is a result of hormonal secretions which are not eliminated properly.

Yoga as well as ayurveda says that if you are able to regulate the timing of your meals, the body will create a system for itself where the digestive juices will flow out at a specific time and clear the system. Therefore, whether you eat three times a day or five times a day does not matter as long as you maintain a regular timing. In the ashram we eat three times a day: breakfast, lunch and dinner, with a bit of tea thrown in for the glucose high. People are not used to this routine, so they are uncomfortable with it. However, in the long run, this is one of the best systems that can be adopted to improve the quality of one's life and health.

Regular sleep pattern: Similarly, to have a regular sleep pattern is important. There can be exceptions, but generally, try to sleep and wake up at specific times. Too much sleep or sleep deprivation are both bad for the brain and mind. When you are able to regulate your sleep pattern, the brain and mind will be charged with the right power, shakti, quality and guna.

If you try and are able to cultivate restraint and discipline in the path of pravritti, the path of enjoyment of the senses and sense objects, that will become your sadhana and attainment. You will be able to live the pravritti path in a better and happier manner, without feeling frustrated, dejected or depressed. You will be able to live your life with optimism and with a smile.

Path of nivritti

The other path is that of nivritti, away from worldly experience and sensory experience. It is a path in which you become intently and intensely aware of your inner spirit and inner or spiritual dimensions of experience.

Nivritti means lessening of vrittis. It is a path where the vrittis become less and less, and gradually subside; the high peaks of vrittis become flat. You are not looking for an absence of vrittis, but management of vrittis. In the pravritti or external path, the spikes of vrittis are hard and sharp and take you to extremes of reactions and responses, while in the nivritti path the spikes of vrittis disappear and become a flat line. They don't have any hold or sway on your mind and you are able to witness the play of vrittis as a *drashta*, observer or seer. You are able to cultivate a transcendental vritti which is not material or gross, known as *brahmi vritti*, the transcendental mentality.

The word brahma is symbolic of the Supreme Spirit. The Supreme Spirit is genderless, and the word brahma is also neither feminine nor masculine. It comes from the root *brinh*, which means that which is continually expanding; therefore, *brahma* means the higher state which is continually evolving. The brahmi vritti is thus a state of consciousness which is free of material bondages; it does not carry any impression of the material existence, it is an internal state of freedom.

Whether you follow the material vritti or the brahmi vritti, you must use the body, mind, senses and intellect when you exist in the world. The instruments of life are the same for a bhogi as well as a yogi. The difference between the two is seen in their mentality. A bhogi likes to remain engrossed in the world and desires the pleasures of the world, whereas a yogi does not desire the pleasures of the world but searches for the bliss of the self. The yogi does not wish to attach with the world, but tries to connect with the transcendental element.

When you live in society, you are always attaching yourself with others, as these connections give you recognition, name, fame, position and status. In the path of nivritti, you gradually free yourself from the bondages of the world and remain free. You remain in the world, but are free of the world. The scriptures give the example of a lotus in water. Just as a lotus grows in swamps but no drop of water is able to settle on it, so should be human life. This is an indication to walk the path of nivritti. To do so, to come to the point of experiencing the transcendental nature or mentality, you have to subject yourself to the cultivation of three powers.

Three powers of nivritti

The first power of the nivritti path is *tyaga* or renunciation. The second is *samarpan* or dedication. The third is *vishwas* or belief. Renunciation, dedication and belief are the tools of the nivritti path.

The path of nivritti is the opposite to that of pravritti. Imagine that there is a road going from north to south. When you are walking towards the north on that road, your back is to the south. You cannot see the southern direction, you can only see ahead in the northern direction. If you want to go south, you will have to turn around so that your back is to the north and face to the south, and start walking southwards. This is true of the paths of pravritti and nivritti also. They are exact opposites of each other.

In the path of pravritti you are facing the world; in nivritti you turn your back to the world. In pravritti you turn your back to the divine, in nivritti you look at the divine and turn your back to the world. This is where people fail to realize the difficulty of the spiritual journey. In order to turn away from the world there has to be total disconnection, which people are unable to achieve. I have seen people who, instead of turning around, begin to walk backwards and say, "I'm going towards nivritti and gradually distancing myself from the world." The concept of distancing does not apply in spiritual life. It is either yes or no, black or white. There is no grey in between. There is either sunlight or darkness.

When somebody asked Buddha, "How can we know that we are progressing in spiritual life?" Buddha replied, "The only indication of progress in spiritual life is a reduction of desires, a reduction of obsessions and aspirations." All these gradually lessen as you walk the spiritual path; they cease to have any hold on you. When that happens, know that you are becoming free of the gross vrittis which hold the mind and bind it to the world of senses. Use this opportunity to cultivate the brahmi vritti. Therefore, the three stages of spiritual life or the nivritti path – renunciation, dedication and belief – have to be understood in the right perspective.

Ladder of tyaga

The disconnection, renunciation or tyaga being spoken of here is a simple process. It is not an intellectual method; you don't think, 'I must leave this.' When you go up a ladder, your feet automatically leave the lower rungs. First you get a firm hold on the next step and then let go of the lower step. This is tyaga, and it is possible only when you hold on to something better. If you want to discard a negative attribute, first get hold of something positive. Establish yourself in positivity and negativity will be automatically left behind. If you turn tyaga into an intellectual thought of 'From today I am going to cast this off', you will not be able to do so. Many people have tried it and have been unsuccessful.

What is there to renounce? It is not possible to renounce the external world because everyone is part of the same environment. Even a saint cannot renounce the world. How can anyone renounce the world when they are unable to renounce the body, the senses, the mind, the feelings and emotions, the beliefs and intellect, the samskaras and karmas? What is the meaning of renouncing home and hearth? Nothing. You can leave behind your home, family, friends and country, but they cannot be renounced. They can be left behind until the journey of your life brings you back to the same spot. You have left them behind for a limited time, but you have not renounced them.

What you need to renounce is the obsessions of the mind. That is the most difficult renunciation, the most difficult tyaga. How do you renounce your obsessive desires and thoughts, your tamasic nature? To find the answer, tyaga must be seen from a different perspective. Not as renunciation of something, but as attainment of something better. With such attainment, that which is useless will automatically be left behind. That is why, when you begin your journey on the path of nivritti, you need to first know and understand yourself. You have to first identify your samskaras and karmas.

Nivritti is a path on which you are nobody's friend or companion. I told you the story of Atmaram. He made many friends in the hotel, Ms Desire, Miss Understanding, Mr Pride, Mr Avarice. The manager of the hotel, Moneyram, also had many companions. However, when The Guide came to the hotel, everyone said, "He lives alone. He does not interact with anyone or talk to anyone. He is happy on his own." The residents could not even meet The Guide, as he would always remain locked in his room.

Think about it. If you have to keep yourself free from envy, like, dislike, attachment and desire, and experience inner balance, peace and joy, what would you have to do? You would have to disassociate from all these things. If you spend all your time with Miss Desire, all you will see is desire. If your friend is Mr Pride, you will remain immersed in pride. The more you remain engrossed in the world, the more this horde of worldly figures will rule over you. You have to make the effort to become free of the worldly vrittis, and there is only one way of doing that.

It is often stated in history and in stories that people renounce society and go into solitude in forests, mountains and caves so they can practise spiritual sadhana. However, can this step transform someone who has been following the pravritti path all along into a person who now follows the nivritti path? Wisdom and experience say no, because it is very easy to renounce the external things, but the threads that bind internally are very difficult to cut off. How can they be cut off? In the presence of the guru.

Guru: brain and heart surgeon

The strength to follow the nivritti path is obtained with the help of a guru. A guru is not a spiritual teacher. In the absence of an appropriate word or proper understanding, the word *guru* is equated with teacher, but its literal meaning is 'dispeller of darkness'. It does not mean teacher or master, but one who sheds light upon the dark confines of your nature. The guru is the agent of inspiration and shows the method by which you can understand renunciation, dedication and belief.

The guru is both brain and heart surgeon. As brain surgeon, the guru tells you to observe your own mind and nature, and finely tweak the mind and personality. If there is negativity, the guru may say, "Don't be so negative, think of something positive." The follower may, under the sway of the negative influence, ignore the mandate of the guru and be carried away by the negative force and continue to scream,

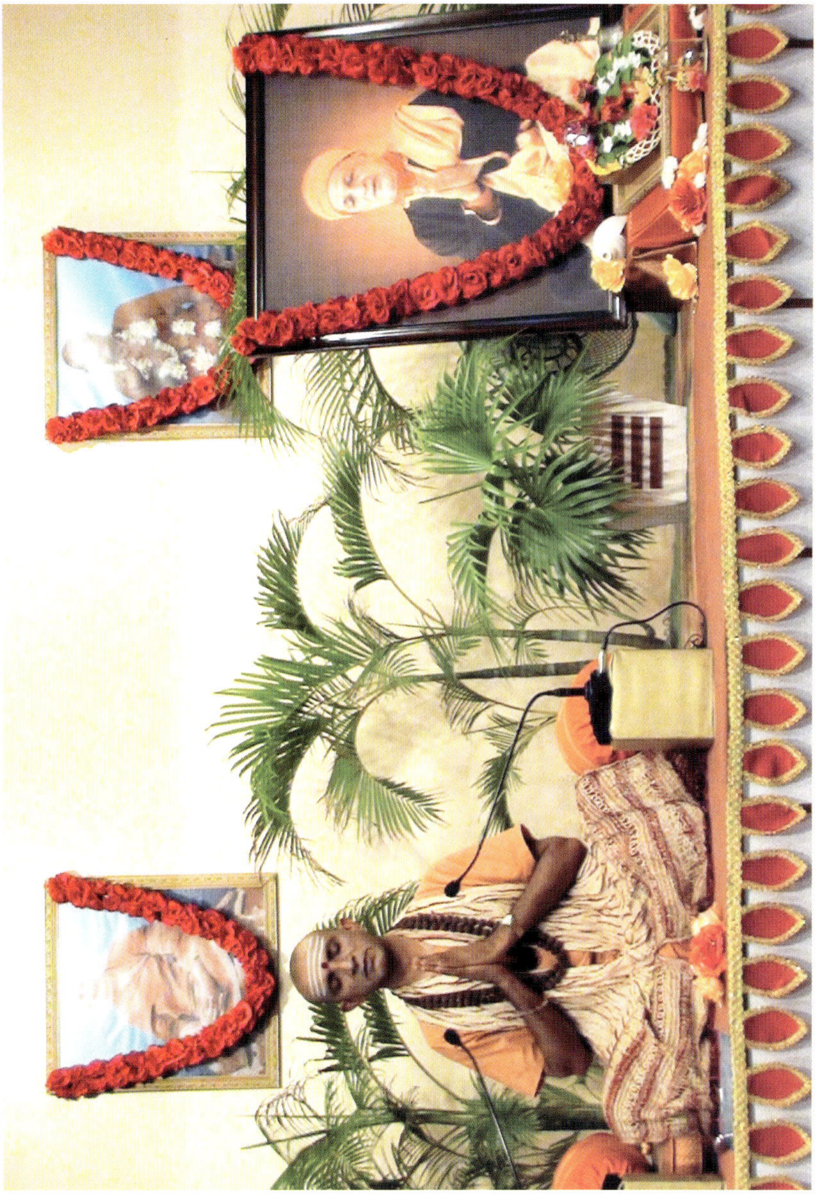

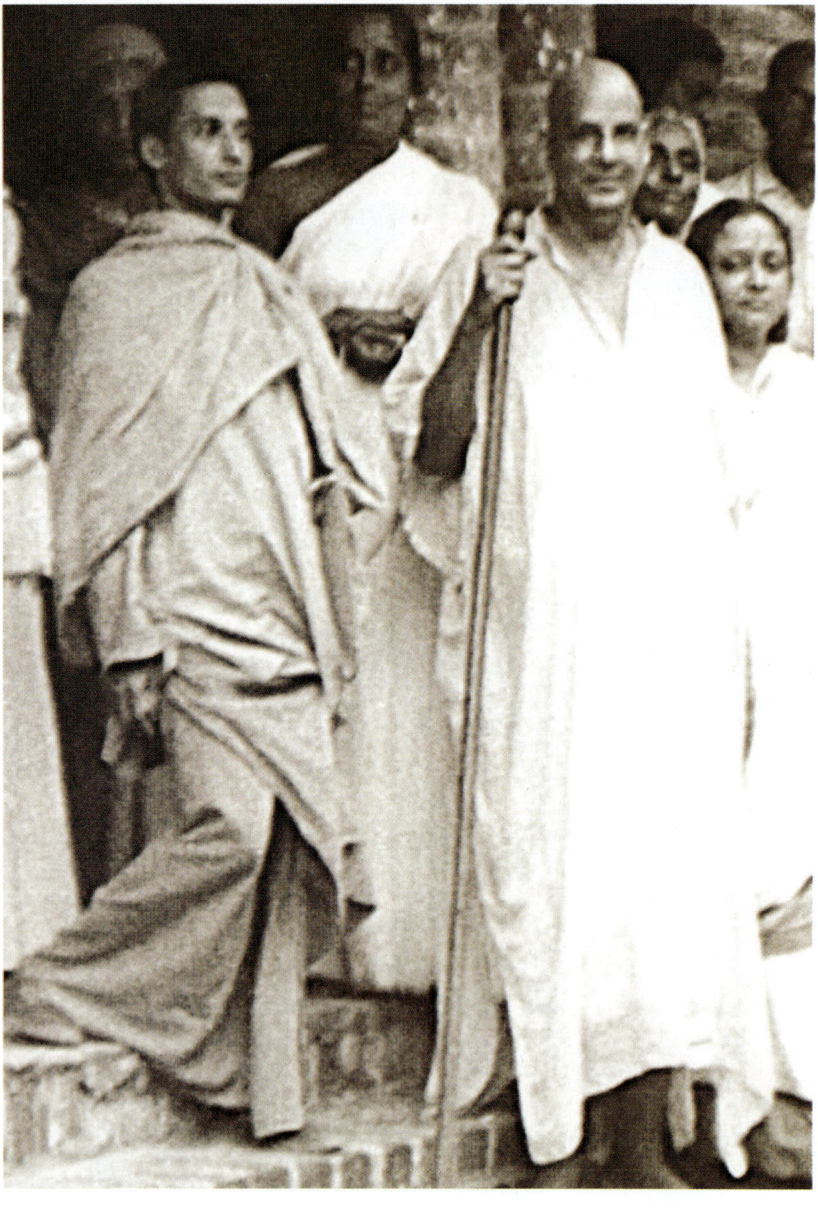

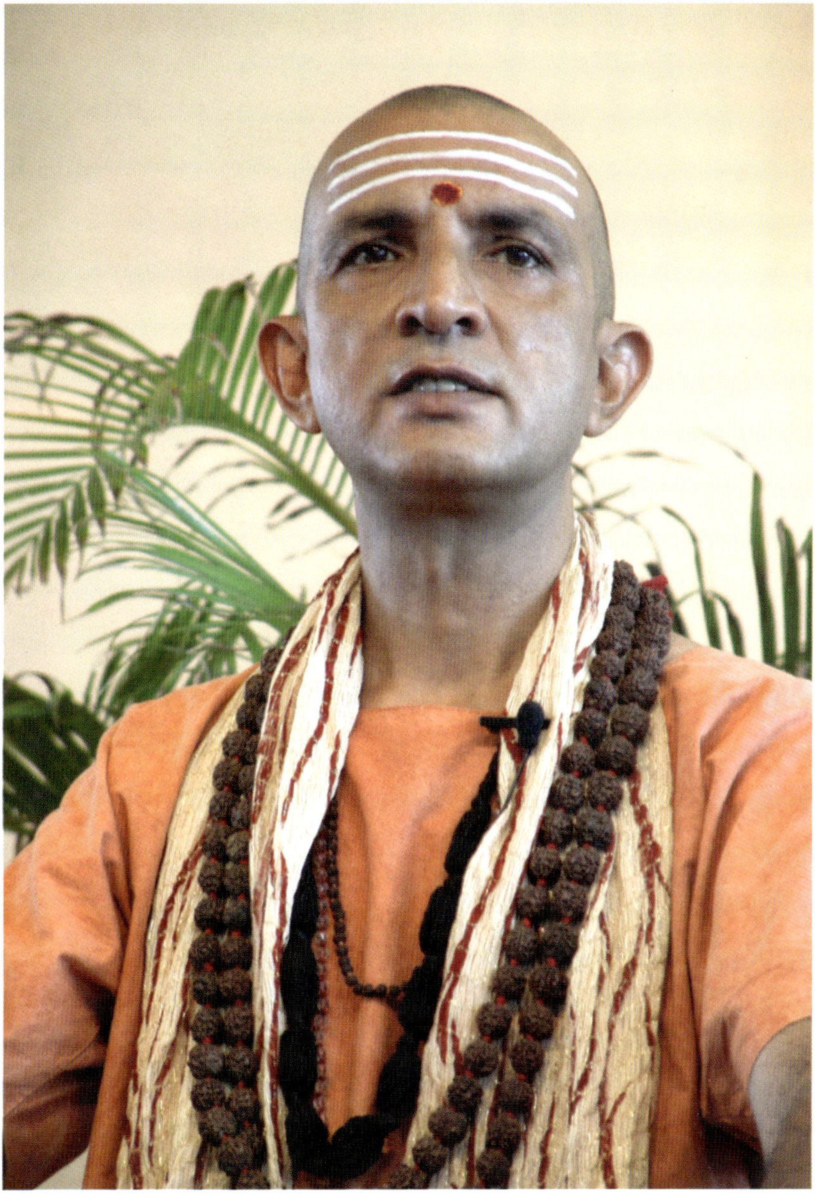

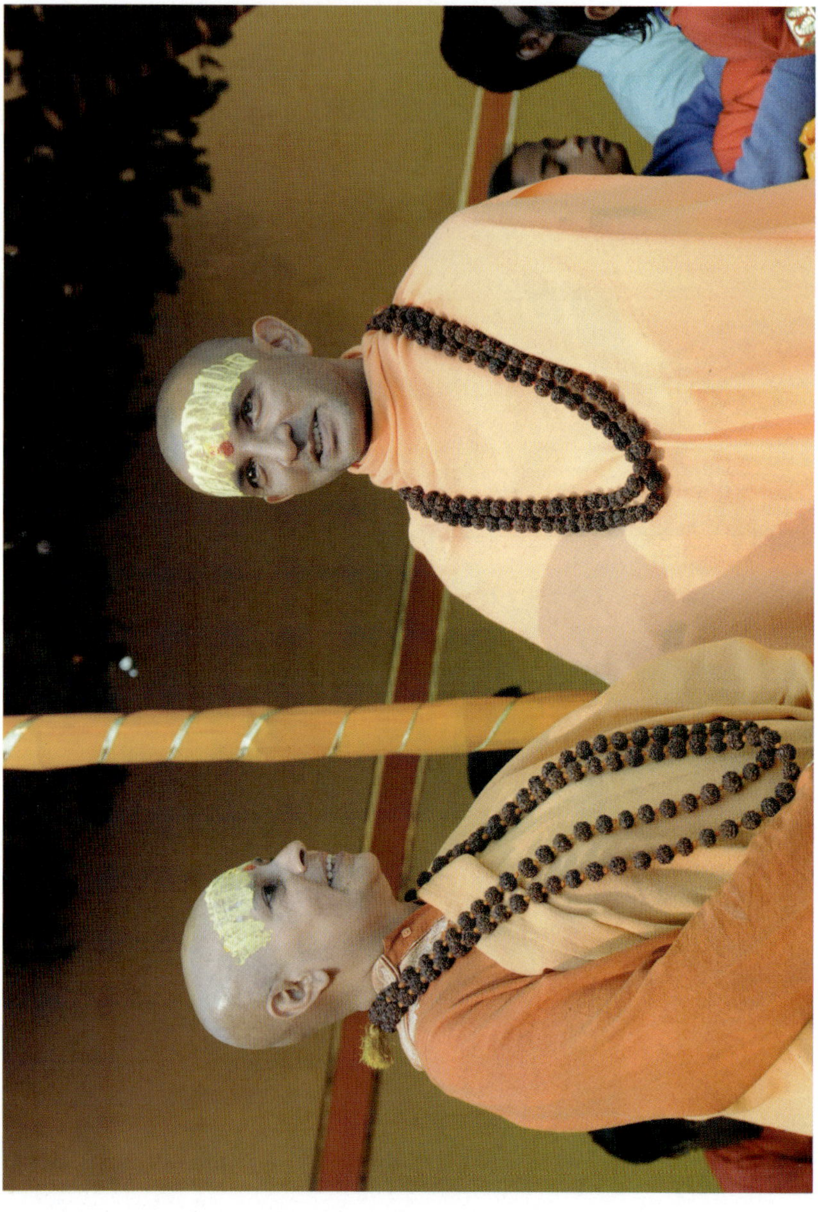

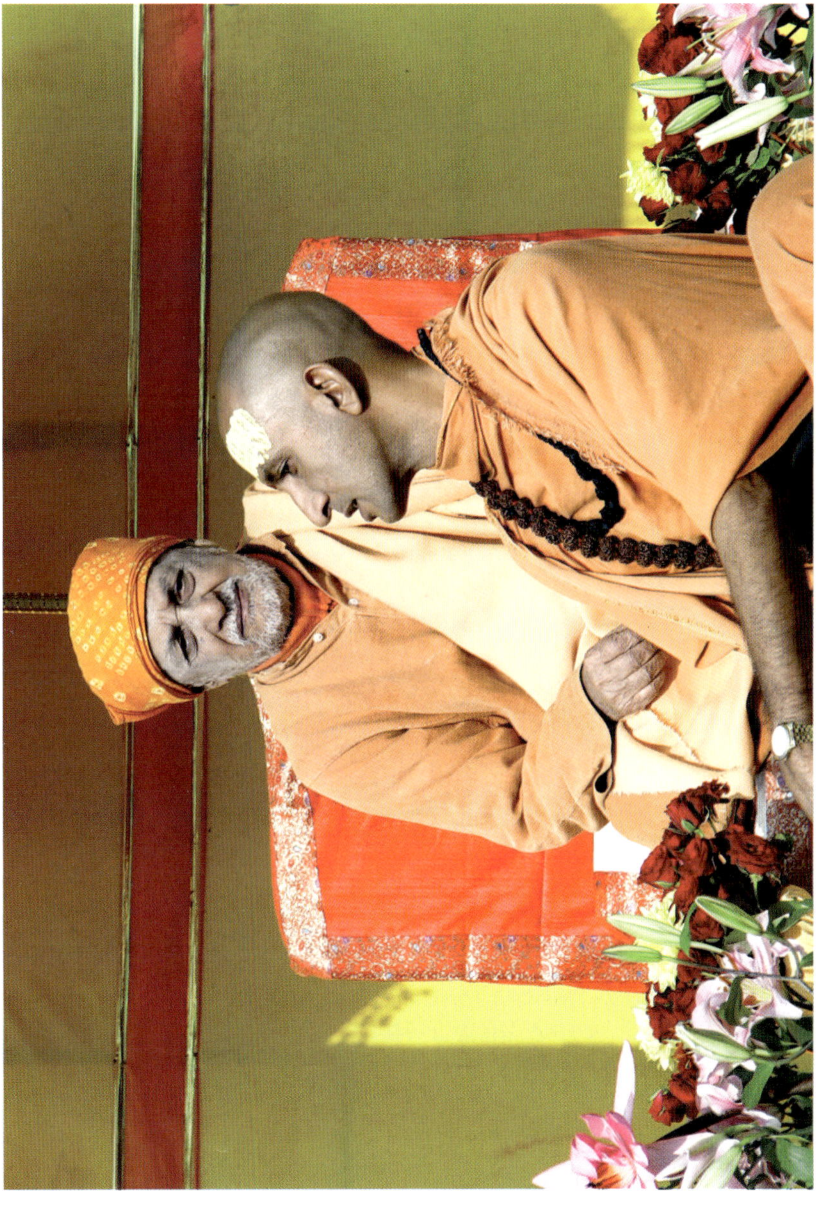

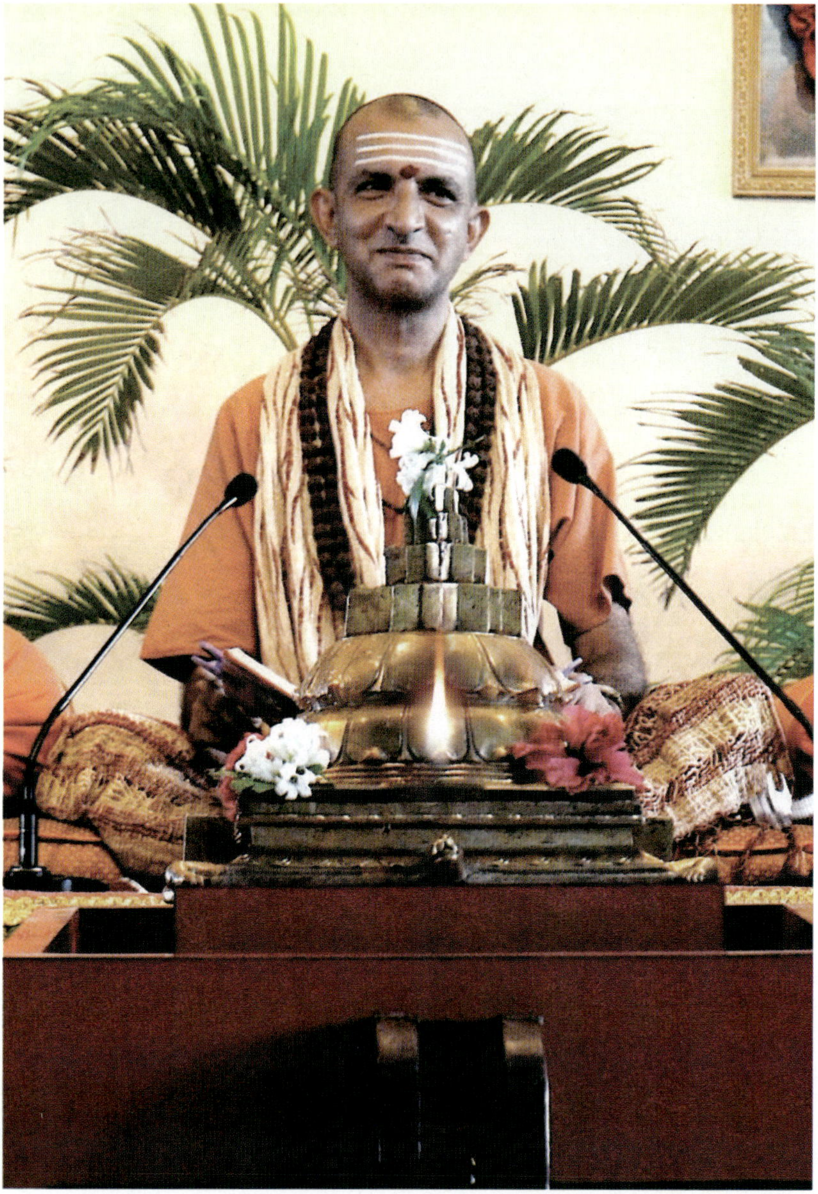

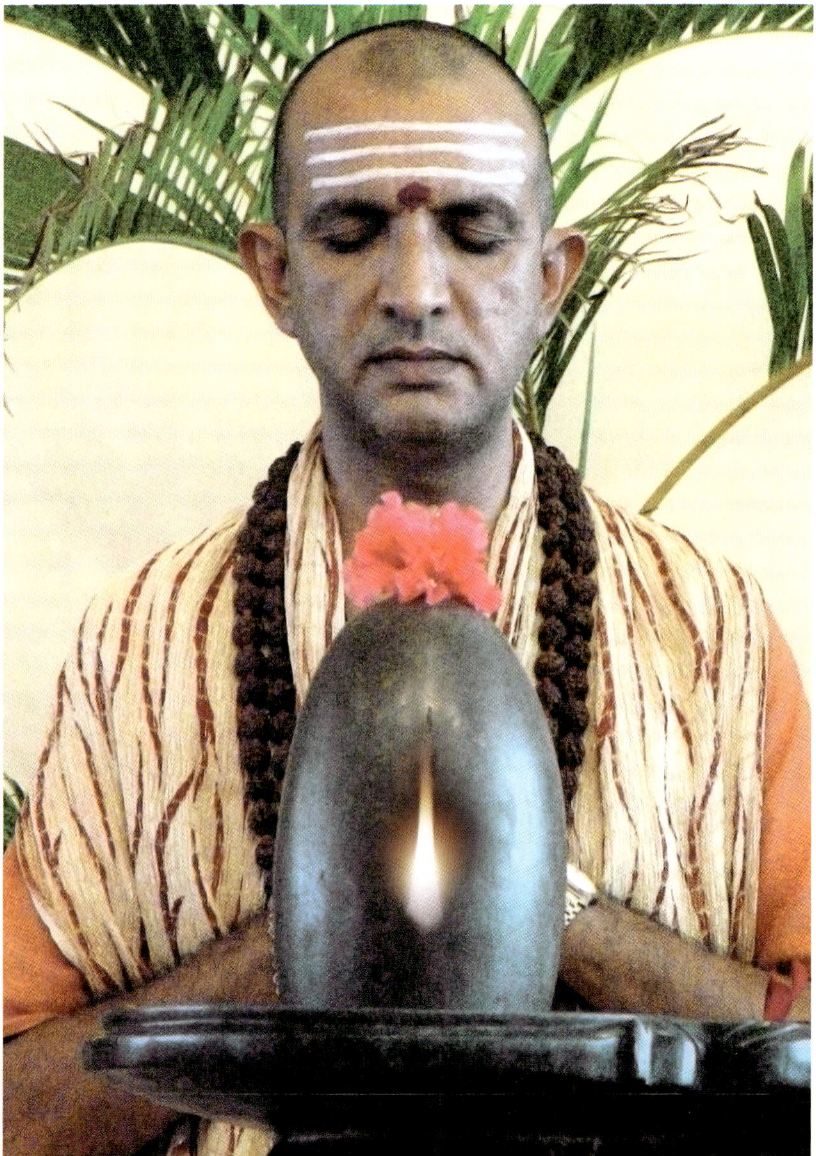

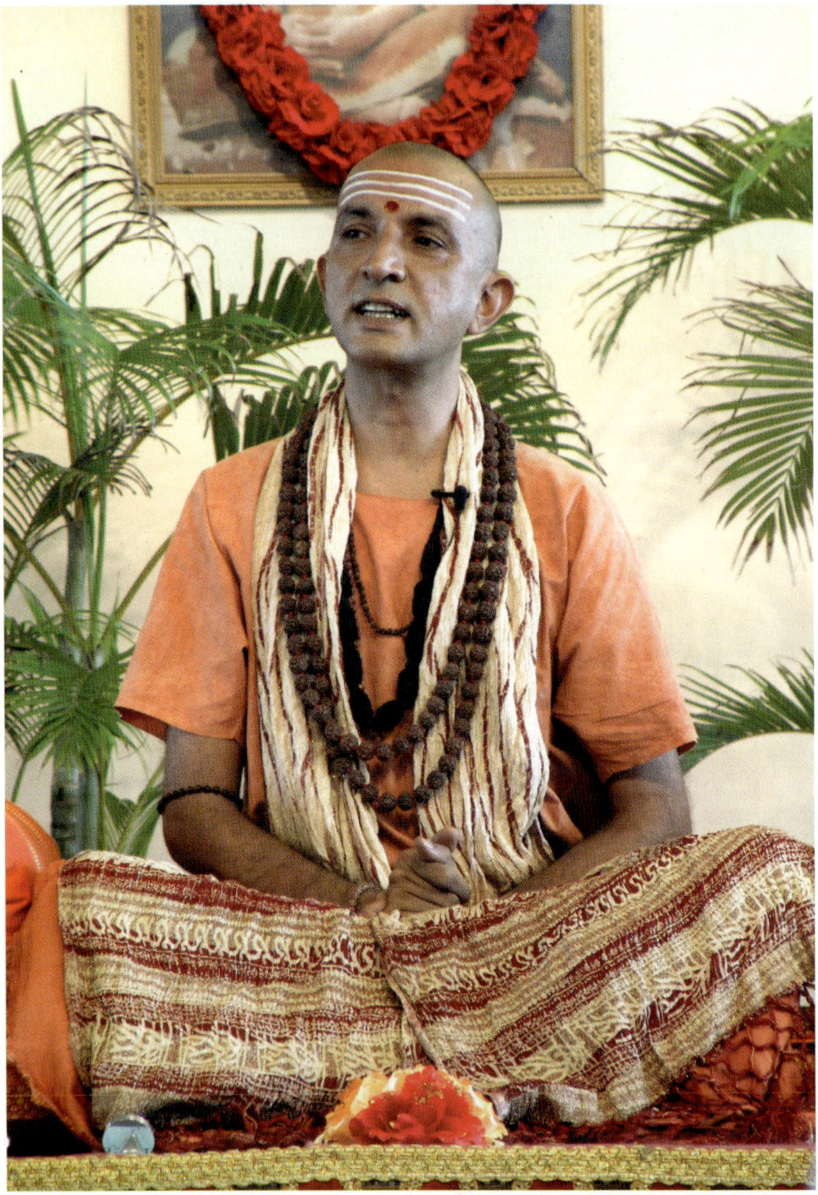

yell, shout and fight. The guru has shown you the way by saying, "Stop fighting, stop struggling, think of something nice, think of connecting yourself with people rather than alienating from people." If you can follow that guideline, you will improve. If you ignore it, you will continue to be in the same rut. Therefore, the guru is the brain or mind surgeon. Due to his teachings, input and inspiration, it is possible to bring about a positive change in the functions of the mind and behaviour.

In 1995, the first Sat Chandi Yajna was held in Rikhia. It was the first major function in Rikhia. We were all very active and I was in the thick of things. When the program started and the Sat Chandi pooja commenced, Sri Swamiji called me and said, "You will sit in that pooja." I said, "How is that possible? You know that I have so many things to do and look into. You want me to sit in the pooja! How can I manage that?" He said, "Just sit in the pooja and forget everything else." I sat down and I had to tweak my mind intensely to bring it back from all the places it was running to, bring it back to the pooja and hold it there. I found that because I had trust and belief in my guru, I was able to do that instantly. Within a minute I became totally focused and centred, and forgot everything else that I was involved in. Nothing bothered me any more. Only for one moment the thought had come, "How am I going to manage it!" but then belief took over and I said to myself, "If my guru wants, it will happen." It did happen.

If you allow the guru to tweak your mind, then you can overcome many mental problems and difficulties that you face in life because of maladjustment, misunderstanding or mistakes – those friends in Hotel Samsara.

The guru is also a heart surgeon. First, he performs surgery on the mind, bringing in positivity, optimism, hope and clarity, and the second surgery is on the heart. After the head is clear, he connects your heart with the divine. Therefore, the first role of the guru is as head surgeon and the second is as heart surgeon. When he performs surgery on your heart, you are freed from the selfish nature and acquire a selfless quality. You rise above selfishness. All the past conditionings of life come to an end, all differences cease to exist, and such a disciple says,

Ishwara, Allah, Vahe Guru, chaahe kaho Sri Rama;
Maalik sab ka eka hai, alag alag hai naam.

Call Him Ishwara, Allah, Vahe Guru or Sri Rama;
Many are the names, but the lord of all beings is one.

All differences come to an end. If the heart surgery is not performed, you keep regretting your shortcomings. That is why a guru is needed. The disciple who allows the guru to have access to his or her life is able to follow the nivritti path, in which tyaga or renunciation, samarpan or dedication, and vishwas or belief become the forces which propel one forward in the journey and discovery of the transcendental nature.

Guru's Guidance

26 June 2010

The two paths that you encounter in life are the paths of pravritti and nivritti. In the pravritti path there is intense involvement of the senses, the self and the world. Three things are involved here: the self, the senses which are the medium of involvement, and the world. It is a path where there is intense entanglement of the senses and sense objects, of the vrittis which are associating with the outer sense objects. In this situation, in order to gain balance and equilibrium, mental stability and inner harmony, and cultivate an appropriate nature through which you can become aware of higher experiences, the process of restraint and discipline has been defined. Sanyam and anushasana constitute the sadhana of the pravritti path. Sanyam is attained with restraint of the senses, mind and speech, and anushasana is attained with regular practice of mantra, yoga, and modification of diet and sleep patterns.

The foundation of the nivritti path is renunciation or *tyaga*, dedication or *samarpan* and belief or *vishwas*. These three are to be found within with the help of a guide, a guru. Their attainment in the real sense becomes possible when there is openness with the guru. In the nivritti path, the guidance of a guru is imperative, but even the harmony that is sought in the pravritti path becomes easier to attain with the help of a guru.

Guidance in the path of pravritti

Brain surgeon: How does the guru guide in the pravritti path? You are already living in pravritti; therefore, there is no need to guide you to it, but there is a need to modify your interaction with *prakriti* or nature, environment and society.

To do this, the guru has to work on you at the mental level. When the guru works on the mental level, he becomes the mind surgeon or brain surgeon. Everyone is facing certain conditions of the mind at their given mental level. Everyone, whether a saint or a sinner, faces dissipation of the mental forces, distractions, anxiety, frustration and desire to fulfil aspirations. The guru only modifies your way of thinking, so that instead of a pessimistic view of life, you are able to develop an optimistic view. Instead of feeling helpless, you begin to experience hope. Instead of feeling dejected, you experience inspiration and motivation. The guru helps you to achieve this by fine-tuning your mind and guiding you through an understanding of what you are reacting to in life.

The first task of the guru is to transform the deluded, narrow and negative thoughts of the disciple. In the life of a disciple, transformation of thinking needs to come about first, then follows transformation of emotions. You perceive the world through your thoughts and you can also perceive your spirit through your thoughts. Thoughts are the medium through which you can see the world and also reach the transcendental reality; they can take you both towards the world and God. Therefore, the guru's first task is to transform the disciple's thought process so it is possible to perceive the positive aspects of life. This is how mental transformation comes about. The guru shows you how to look at yourself, the world and God from a different perspective.

The first requirement is surgery on the brain, fine-tuning the mental behaviour in order to acquire a better perspective, knowledge, attitude and understanding, enabling smoother integration with society, family and environment. If the aspirant, whether a grihastha or renunciate, is able to understand and pick up these messages and teachings of the guru, then the positive and creative forces of the mind are allowed the opportunity to manifest. Once the positive potentials of the mind manifest, there is balance, harmony and integration of the various human faculties. In this manner, you are able to develop a positive and balanced attitude towards life and society. By developing a better understanding of yourself, you integrate in society and the family in a better way. There is greater fulfilment and happiness, and development of a connection which is pure and innocent.

There are people who stop after reaching this point in life. The need for a guru in their life is only to fine-tune the mental awareness, and they do not feel the need or necessity to have a guru for another stage of life.

Heart surgeon: The other stage in life is surgery on the heart. There is a group which wants to explore beyond the mind and come closer to their spiritual nature. For such people the guru becomes the heart surgeon. Once the mind becomes peaceful and balanced, there comes transformation of emotions. After having worked through the mind, the guru works with the disciple's sentiments and emotions. The guru becomes the centre in which the normal human emotions can be channelled and focused.

The human emotions are expressions of vital energy, *prana shakti*, which is subtle and uncontrolled. It is the raw form of prana which you experience at the time of an emotional outburst over which there is no intellectual control or understanding, no instinctive control or understanding. It just happens. The outburst, the explosion of raw prana just happens. Depending on what the mind is associating with at that moment, a corresponding response is evoked. If the mind is encountering a threat, the explosion of prana will be felt in the form of fear and anxiety. If it is encountering a pleasant experience, the explosion will evoke a different response. In this manner, depending on where the mind is attached at a particular moment, an emotional response is experienced. This happens every second of your life at an unconscious level. You are constantly responding emotionally to different situations and influences. However, in the presence of the guru, you consciously direct your emotional energies to focus on one point which represents your fulfilment. That one point is internal; you are directing the emotions inwards, away from the experiences of the world into your inner spiritual dimension.

The process which is adopted to guide these emotions in the inner spiritual dimension is bhakti. That is the process to direct the emotional pranic forces inwards. Bhakti is experienced by living with the guru; it is the way to open up the heart. It is said that the first step in perfecting bhakti is association with pious or good people: *Prathama bhagati santana kara sanga*. This means associating with pious and positive people who will uplift your mind, consciousness and pranas. If you associate with critical and negative people, you are not a bhakta. You cannot be a devotee or allow the guru to perform surgery on you. The first condition of bhakti is associating with pious, virtuous, good and positive people. It indicates that associations are very important. They can sway you in the wrong direction or take you in the right direction.

In the first step of positive association, faith must develop. When you associate with someone who you feel can inspire, uplift and guide you, a level of trust must be there. The connection with the guru is that of trust and faith. Trust and faith are awakened when you follow the first condition of bhakti: association with the right people. This provides a new and better understanding and perception about yourself and where you stand. Your direction in life becomes clearer, aspirations become clearer, blockages are removed and misunderstandings are dispelled. This is the beginning of heart surgery.

The guru teaches how to open your heart in order to connect with the transcendental nature that exists everywhere. That is not an intellectual understanding; it is a realization:

Siya Rama maya saba jaga jaani, karahun pranaam jori juga paani.

The whole world as Sita-Rama I know; joining both hands, in obeisance I bow.

It is a realization that everyone is made of the same substance, the same essence. The body is made up of the five elements. People may look different externally, but the basic component which has created everybody is the same, whether you are Indian, American, Russian, Chinese, Japanese or European. The guru imparts the awareness of this connection which exists at the higher level, the inner or spiritual level. Every individual is connected with every other individual and also with the higher transcendental self. When this realization dawns, a change comes about at the emotional level. The emotions which until now were connected only with yourself, with the sense of 'I', no longer remain limited but connect with everyone. You rise above the limits of selfishness, free yourself from the bondage of selfishness and attain a state of mind where no desires remain. Existence of desires means birth of the selfish vritti and cessation of desires means destruction of the selfish vritti. As the intensity of the selfish vritti lessens, the heart becomes purer and crookedness and deviousness disappear from life. The mind and emotions attain purity. A greater appreciation of life takes place.

The guru continues to work his wonders by performing heart surgery. Some people are able to undergo this surgery and become better followers and disciples of the guru's life and teachings. Up to this point, the teachings are common to both a householder and a sannyasin. A worldly person needs to purify the mind and emotions by following the instructions of the guru and so does a renunciate. The householder is satisfied to have reached this point. He thinks 'I have found a guru, and due to guru's compassion I have found God's grace. Having found the grace of God, my mind has become peaceful, my emotions which were earlier limited to myself have become expansive, and due to the purity of mind and emotions I am able to experience joyous and positive conditions in my personality.' The connection of a householder with the guru is limited to this point and their journey stops here.

Guidance in the path of nivritti

There are others, the exceptions, who want to go even further in their spiritual journey and want to become established in the highest spiritual truth. They become sannyasins and follow the nivritti path. In the pravritti path, one may or may not follow a guru, but the journey of the nivritti path begins in the proximity of a guru. In our story, Atmaram started the journey from Hotel Samsara with the help of The Guide, because without a guide's help one cannot become free of pravritti. You may want to do so, you may feel that 'I have been through too much, now I need some peace', but you will not know the way. Therefore, the guru becomes necessary.

A sannyasin is a person who has surrendered to the teachings of the guru and is trying to mould his or her life as per those teachings. Sannyasa has been described as a tradition, and it is indeed that. It has been described as a state of mind, and it is that also. However, the feeling that a disciple experiences at the time of receiving sannyasa is 'I am surrendering myself to my guru, I am eager to realize the teachings of my guru.' As long as you can walk that path, in surrender to guru, realizing the teachings of the guru, the guru guides you to experience the state of tyaga, to flow in surrender and have firm belief. This is where an inner relationship between guru and disciple is formed. The guru helps you understand the foundations of the nivritti path: tyaga, samarpan and vishwas, and to live them.

Teachings to leave excess baggage: Tyaga is generally translated as renunciation, but tyaga should mean gaining and losing. Not renouncing, but gaining and then losing. What is the meaning of the word tyaga, or what is the understanding that comes with the word renunciation? Generally, they convey the idea that you have to leave something behind. It is easy to leave behind home and family, and it is true that a sannyasin must forsake those connections. It has been prescribed that a sannyasin must be free of the bondages of home and family. Tyaga does not mean renunciation here, but freeing oneself from those connections. All parents have certain expectations of their children, and it is necessary to become free of them when you want to follow your own path.

Sri Swamiji tells us that when he was a boy, his father would say, "When you grow up, become a big police officer, join the IPS." That was because he was himself a police officer. His mother was a follower of Mahatma Gandhi and found joy in serving society, so she would say, "Become a social worker when you grow up, forget the police." His aunt would say, "Forget social work. Become a doctor. Then you will be able to look after anyone who falls sick in the family and also serve the poor." In this way, everyone would give their suggestions. He listened to them all for months and years, and finally decided, "I will do none of what these people say. I will become what I want to," and he took sannyasa.

Sri Swamiji tells this story as a joke, but there are expectations in every family. This leads them to exert pressure, with which comes manipulation. Therefore, if you take to the path of sannyasa and want to advance on the spiritual journey, it is necessary to break free of all these relationships. How can you be free of worldly relationships? If you stay together, the connections will continue to be there. That is why you need to leave them. When you don't live together, no connections will be formed. When there is no connection, there will not be any expectation. When there is no expectation, there will not be any pressure. When there is no pressure, you are free. Thus, the spiritual tradition says that a person who wants to move forward on the path of sannyasa must break the connections with home and family. All the same, it is an external process.

When I was a young boy, I would say to Sri Swamiji, "Why do we live in a city? Sadhus are supposed to live in forests and mountains. We should also go to some such place, make an ashram there and live in solitude." Sri Swamiji would reply, "One can live anywhere, a city or forest. But remember, there is no peace in the mountains and there is no noise in the market. All this is a play of your own mind. If you can bring your mind under control, you will find the same peace in the middle of a marketplace which you are searching for in the Himalayas. If you cannot bring your mind under control, then you will not be at peace even in a cave in the Himalayas."

As a child I could not really understand this, but now, one is able to understand that all this is indeed a play of the mind, whether the mind connects with home and family, the senses or objects of sense enjoyment.

This is where the guru imparts the teaching of tyaga. He says, "Leave behind that which is of no value to you."

What has to be left behind is the excess baggage. Are you able to do that? It is very difficult. I haven't yet found a person who is capable of doing this. People always carry the excess baggage of their vasanas, desires and ambitions with them, even in the form of memory. The memory of the good and the bad that you have undergone in life is retained till the end of your days. You are not able to clear this excess baggage from the mind.

Association with the guru teaches how to leave behind the excess baggage – by accepting it. He teaches you to accept that it is there and realize that it has no value and meaning in your life. When you receive something of value, then that which is of no value is automatically left behind. That is tyaga: first gaining something of value and then leaving that which has no value. You have to replace what you give up with something new that you take in. Therefore, tyaga actually means equipping yourself with the appropriate, the best, the optimistic and the positive, and leaving behind the detrimental, the bad, the negative and the destructive. That is the real meaning of the word tyaga, and the guru can guide you towards it by pointing out the shortcomings of your nature. This enables you to experience tyaga over a period of time. This is what I have realized through the training received from Sri Swamiji. What he taught over forty years ago has prepared us to know the difference between *sangraha*, accumulation, and tyaga, renunciation, which may not have been possible otherwise.

Once during Sri Swamiji's days in Rishikesh, Swami Sivananda was making his rounds of the rooms in the ashram and he came to Sri Swamiji's room. There he saw that on the floor was one tiny blanket, and papers, files and pens all over the room. He asked Swami Satyananda, "Where is your bed?" Sri Swamiji said, "That blanket is my bed. I sleep on it. When I feel cold, I cover myself with it." Swami Sivananda said, "Not good enough." He said, "Where is your tea and kettle?" Swamiji said, "I don't need those things. Why should I keep a kettle, tea and sugar in my room? Everything that I need is provided for in the ashram." Swami Sivananda went back to his room and after about fifteen minutes, the accommodation team of the ashram came in with a bed, mattress, pillow, bed sheets, blankets, kettle, tea, stove and kerosene. Sri Swamiji immediately went to Swami Sivananda and said, "What have you done? Why have you sent all those things to my room? I don't require them." Swami Sivananda said, "You may not require them. I have not sent them for you. I have sent them for those who come to your room. If somebody comes to your room at night and it is freezing cold outside, you can make some tea and give it to that person. It will warm him. You can give him a blanket and he will feel warm. These things are not for you; they are for the visitors who come to your room." Sri Swamiji accepted his guru's words and went back.

Now imagine yourself in his place. You would have been so happy thinking, "My guru is looking after me. My guru has given me the sanction to have tea in my room. My guru has sent me a stove and now I can have tea whenever I like." That will be your attitude. Am I wrong? You will feel so happy that Guruji is looking after you and has given you the permission to have tea as many times as you like. But look at the attitude of Swami Sivananda and Swami Satyananda. Swami Sivananda said, "Don't use it for yourself. Keep it for somebody in need." Sri Swamiji also took the instruction in the same manner. He did not think, "I am the favourite of Swami Sivananda now. He has sent me a bed, blankets, bed sheets. I must be his favourite disciple!"

I have related this incident to indicate an important point. You can have everything, but not use it, crave it or desire it. It may not be useful to you, but it will be of use to some other person. This is the concept of tyaga. "It is not my need and I am not even attracted to it. It is there, fine. It has been kept here. At the appropriate time, it will be used." This is a gross example where you have everything and at the same time hold the *bhavana*, feeling, of tyaga, of not needing anything. There is no rejection, there is acceptance. Gradually, you begin to receive spiritual jewels at other levels of life, and the material stones keep on falling away. As you replace the material stones with spiritual jewels, your bag becomes full of jewels and empty of stones. Therefore, leaving something behind is not tyaga, but gaining something of value first and then leaving behind that which is of no value is tyaga.

This is how the teaching of tyaga begins. Leave your obsessive desires behind, become aware of them and then free yourself of them. Break your attachment to sense objects. As you go on severing your connection with sense objects and leaving them behind, as you go on becoming aware of the world and your desires and free yourself of them, you advance on the path of tyaga. However, tyaga is successful only when you receive and then discard. People become afraid of the word tyaga, thinking that they will have to renounce this and that, because they do not want to let go of anything. I gave the example of climbing a ladder: you let go of one step only when your feet are firmly established on the next one. First there is attainment, then letting go.

When the mind becomes healthy, the unhealthy mental conditions are automatically left behind. When the emotions are healthy, then emotional ill-health is left behind. Therefore, the definition of tyaga is not discarding. Its definition is: attain one thing and in its place let go of something, create one connection and free yourself of another connection. This effort must be made continuously in the life of a disciple.

Freedom from mind: The second aspect of the nivritti path is surrender, *samarpan*. *Sam* means total, and *arpan* means offering, "I offer everything." To whom do you offer everything? You can only offer it to guru or God. These are the only two places where you can offer everything. As for God, you don't know Him, you have never seen Him. The guru is present. The connection with the guru is tangible. When the idea of offering everything comes, the aspirant is without a mind. If the mind was there, it would say, "Retain this, retain that." In the absence of the mind, one can offer everything. This is an indication that in the guru-disciple relationship, the mind has to be bypassed. The mental responses have to be transcended.

You know the story of Milarepa. His guru told him, "I want you to make a hut on top of the mountain by carrying stones from the base of the mountain." For many months Milarepa carried stones and rocks, and finally the hut was ready. The guru went to look at it and said, "I don't like the location of this hut. Carry these stones back to the base of the mountain and make a hut there, using the same rocks and stones." Milarepa again carried the rocks and stones from the top of the mountain to the base, and constructed a hut. His guru, Marpa, again looked at it and said, "No, I don't like this place. I think the top is better. Shift everything back up again."

Any other person would have thought the guru was crazy, but a disciple who had bypassed his mind did not question the whims of the guru's demand. He said to himself, "This is the instruction of my guru. This is what is expected of me. I will do it." Without thinking twice, he simply obeyed. He did not think even once, "Is my guru troubling me? Is he trying to see how I respond, how I behave?" Nothing like that. Milarepa did not go through any head trip at all. He had dedicated and devoted himself completely and had the conviction, "If I have stopped thinking about myself and handed over that responsibility to the guru, then that is the guru's duty. I have nothing to worry about."

When it comes to samarpan, the disciple must think carefully: 'Where do I stand with respect to my surrender?' Samarpan means emptying oneself from within. Arjuna asked Krishna many questions, but Krishna did not reply to them until Arjuna said: *Shishyasteham shaadhi maam twaam prapannam* – "I give my head over to you as your disciple." That is when Krishna started the discourse of the *Bhagavad Gita*, not before that. A guru knows that the inner receptivity of a disciple develops only when there is dedication. It does not develop when you stand rigid and are only focused on expressing your own thoughts. Therefore, samarpan means that you surrender to the guru tattwa or Ishwara tattwa endowed with faith.

Once there were two aspirants who had been practising intense austerities. They had hung themselves upside down from a banyan tree for innumerable years and were doing their sadhana in that posture. One day, Sage Narada was passing by in the sky. Due to the attainments of their sadhana, the two were able to see him. They called out to him. Narada came down and the two also came down from the tree and paid their respects to him. They asked him, "Where are you going?" Narada replied, "You know that I am the official reporter of heaven. I am going to Narayana to interview him." The aspirants said, "Well, if you are going to Narayana, we also have a question for him. Will you ask on our behalf?" Narada asked, "What is the question?" The aspirants replied, "Please ask him when he will come to give us darshan." Narada said, "Okay, no big deal. I will ask."

The two aspirants went back to their tree. A few days later, Narada returned. The aspirants asked eagerly, "Did you ask him our question? What did he say?" Narada said, "Narayana has said that he will certainly give you darshan, but it will take time." The aspirants asked, "How long?" Narada replied, "Narayana said that as many leaves as there are on this tree, it will take him the same number of years to appear before you." The two looked at the tree, it had innumerable leaves. One of them said, "I am not ready to wait for so many years. I am going back home. At least I will be able to eat good food cooked by my wife there instead of roots and berries. I am enduring heat and cold on the tree here; there I will be able to sleep on a soft bed. There is no one to look after me or converse with here. There I will be able to chat with my children and grandchildren." Thinking in this manner, he picked up his bag and left.

The other aspirant thought, "No one till today has been able to know when God will appear before him. God has told me that He will certainly come to me, and He has even given me the time. I have received His assurance." Filled with love for

Narayana, he went back to the tree and continued to perform his sadhana. The moment the thought that 'God has assured me and I will certainly have His darshan' came to his mind, Narayana appeared before him!

Narada became very angry. He said to Narayana, "Lord, you turned me into a liar! Why did you come now? There was no need for you to come now. You had said it would take you thousands of years." Narayana said, "Look Narada, one aspirant thought 'Why should I waste my time?' and went back home. The other one thought 'I have received an assurance from God and He will certainly give me darshan.' As soon as this feeling of faith and surrender came to his mind, the laws of time stopped for him and I had to appear before him."

That level of samarpan, dedication, comes when you are able to cultivate trust and faith. Otherwise, at a certain point in your dedication, you will always stop. The trust and faith are not complete. When you realize that your trust or faith are not complete, your journey will stop, your dedication will stop, your surrender will stop. Therefore, samarpan actually means that you bypass your mind and develop a simple, innocent and humble relationship with your guru. Through the guru, the relationship continues to God.

You can offer faith only to that which is known to you. How can you offer your faith to that which you have not seen, which is unknown to you? Many yogis have contemplated this subject over the ages. Even in the *Bhagavad Gita*, Arjuna asks Krishna (12:1):

Evam satata yukta ye bhaktaastvaam paryupaasate;
Ye chaapyaksharamavyaktam teshaa ke yogavittamaah.

There are two kinds of people who worship you: those who believe in your formless existence and those who worship your form. Who among the two is superior?

Krishna replies, "Both are acceptable to me. Those who worship the formless Me attain Me and those who worship Me in a form also attain Me. Both paths are equally good."

However, it is easier to follow the path of form, as it allows you to focus your mind at one point: your object of worship. As you advance in the path of form, the experience of duality goes away. As you develop faith and surrender, the sense of duality comes to an end and the form turns into the formless. Just as you need steps to go to the roof, you need the help of a form to reach the formless. After all, everything in this world is a form. There is nothing formless in this dimension. How can you then perceive the formless or even think about it? People say that Om is the formless aspect of God, but even Om has a form.

How will you meditate on the formless? Even if you meditate on the breath, it has a form, it is an experience. If you meditate on a mantra, it is a sound, a wave, a form. If you meditate on a flame, that is also a form. 'Formless' is only an idea, but the progression in connection takes place with the help of a form. Whatever you focus your mind on is a form. The effort to connect with the Supreme Element is achieved with the help of a form. It is worship of form that gives birth to faith, and it is with the help of a form that one is able to arrive at surrender. When the mind is not standing rigid on the strength of its obsessive desires, but remains balanced on the strength of its spirit, that is surrender. When the mind is stuck in desires, it walks the path of bhoga. When it is firm in faith, it walks the path of yoga. This is the teaching the guru gives: how to remove the mind from desires and connect it with the spirit. When the guru is able to connect you with your spirit and you experience that connection, then surrender comes to a culmination in life.

Cultivating heartfelt conviction: The third foundation of the nivritti path is vishwas, belief. It is not intellectual knowing, it is heartfelt conviction.

A story in the Upanishads states that once there was a kingdom which was suffering from drought for many years. People were suffering due to lack of water, the land was turning into desert and the citizens were migrating to other places in search of greener pastures. The king consulted the wise men of his kingdom and decided to perform a havan to invoke the rains.

At an auspicious time, a group of learned priests came together and started to perform the ceremony to invoke rain. The havan went on for many months. People from all over the kingdom would come to participate and pray to God for an end to the drought. One day, a young boy came to have darshan of the yajna. He arrived with an open umbrella over his head. Everyone present at the yajna began to make fun of this little boy, saying, "Is it raining that you have come with an umbrella? The sky is blue, the sun is merciless, there is not a single cloud in the sky as far as the eyes can see and you are standing here with an umbrella! Do you think it is going to rain?" The boy replied, "You are performing the yajna for rain, yet you do not believe that your yajna will yield results. I have come from a distant village, believing that with this yajna, rain will come down and the calamity that our kingdom is facing will be averted. I believe rain will come."

When the boy said these words to the priests, they were speechless. They were performing the yajna, but they had no belief in it, whereas the little boy believed that the yajna would yield the right result. He had come with that belief, and as soon as he spoke the words, it started to rain. It rained cats and dogs for days and there was everything in abundance in the kingdom. All because of the belief of one boy who had the heartfelt conviction that what was being done would bring the right result.

That is the power of belief or vishwas. Vishwas is not just believing in something, but also knowing that it will come true.

There is the story of Mother Shabari in *Ramacharitamanas*. When she was about sixteen years old, her guru told her, "One day Rama will come to your hut." He did not tell her when, the date, month or year. From that day onwards, every day Shabari believed, "Today is the day that Rama will arrive at my hut." Every day she would prepare for Rama's arrival, clean her hut, gather fruits, prepare his asana, prepare everything as if an important guest was going to pay a visit. She continued doing this till the ripe old age of eighty. In her eightieth year, Rama came to her home. For seventy-four years, she had been expecting him every day. Would you have had such hope? After three days, you would have said, "Whenever you come, I will deal with you at that time." That would have been your attitude. But for Shabari, her conviction, faith and trust in her guru was intense. The guru had said, "Rama will come to your house one day" and she waited every day of her life with the same patience and intensity. Looking forward to his arrival did not diminish as time went by.

These are some examples of the type of mind you can develop. They are not isolated examples of historical figures. These are conditions of mind which every individual can develop, provided there is the depth of feeling within.

Tyaga, samarpan and vishwas are the three tools with which you can progress on the path of nivritti. As you make progress on this path, the vasanas, obsessions, desires and aspirations lessen, and the mind becomes freer. The chain which binds the mind gradually falls away, and it begins to experience freedom – freedom from vrittis, from involvement in the world of senses and sense objects – and you begin to relive your spiritual, transcendental and transformative nature. You establish a connection with your own self, with God, with guru, and that connection is an eternal connection. Just as the energy of God remains awakened and alive in the guru, the energy of guru becomes awakened and alive in the disciple.

Reaching the destination

These are the two paths of life, pravritti and nivritti. By adopting the principles which we have discussed, it is definitely possible to improve the quality of lifestyle. You don't have to change your lifestyle, you have to improve the quality of your lifestyle. Those who are following the path of pravritti have to create a better system, structure and understanding in their everyday routine, in which the effort to integrate with the outer society along with the cultivation of inner awareness can coexist. For this the methods are anushasana, sanyam and sadhana. While for those following the nivritti path, it is necessary to become endowed with tyaga, samarpan and vishwas, and follow the guidance of a guru. This is how you fulfil the purpose for which you have taken birth: to realize the luminosity within, to complete the journey to the City of Light, Brahmapuri.